CW01429742

JOURNEYS W

By Emelye Jessica Purser

A spiritual self-help guide

Published by

Intuitive Therapy 2024

ISBN 978-17393378-2-7

Copyright Emelye Purser © 2024

40353 words

Email: emelyepurser@hotmail.com

https://sites.google.com/view/21emelyeintuitivetherapy

Facebook: emelyejessica

intuitive therapy

EMELYE PURSER

Contents

Nurture, a watercolour on canvas by Emelye

Copyright

Disclaimer

Please be aware that complementary therapies complement, but do not replace conventional medical treatment and care. No therapist can guarantee specific results. The therapist may give information or guidance in this book for the client to consider. This guidance could bring about positive results where the client is motivated to change, in conjunction with proper medical support if required. Any resulting choices and changes made, remain the personal and also the legal responsibility of the client.

"Journeys with Angels," is to be used for therapeutic guidance and daydreaming.

Acknowledgements

I acknowledge with gratitude the help I have received from Jamie my husband, who took me to explore the beautiful sensory journeys that are described here for you to enjoy.

Our children: Jake, Josie, Ernie, William and George also deserve a warm thanks for joining us on our journeys that have been influenced with their encouragement and infectious enthusiasm that brought their stories to life.

I would also like to thank Geoff O' Neill, an IT Trainer at Action for Blind People, for showing me that technology can be used by those with a visual impairment. Without his help, this book would not have been possible. I would also like to thank Yvonne Brooks, also from Action for Blind People, and The Honeywood Trust, for lending me a laptop that has enabled me to write this book and run a business confidently.

Guide Dogs Mobility Team, Southampton deserve a special thank you, for the dedicated Guide Dog trainers, who gave so much valuable help with yellow Labrador Stella, from 2007. She worked for seven years then took retirement with the family in 2014. She welcomed beautiful black Labrador-Retriever Quaver, into her home. Quaver took over from 2014, also worked for seven years and retired with the family in 2023. My new working partnership with Golden Retriever, Arthur, (who's picture is shown below) began in the summer of 2023. He has the company of Quaver, who is an excellent teacher and friend.

Guide dog Arthur   Guide dog Quaver   Guide dog Stella

Introduction

You never know which journey will be yours today. However, you can be sure that the one that you choose will be right for this time. This is not a book to read from the beginning to the end, instead follow your chosen number to lead you, in an order that is right for you. This book is designed to explore the emotions that are relevant now and to find your very best creative potential.

Close your eyes and reflect on your life as it has been, then open them to see how it is now. When you are ready, pick an angel number between one and forty, turn to that number, and look forwards to the future with compassion and empathy for who you really are.

Angel Numbers

Angel numerology has been recognised as having a timeless spiritual connection, that is understood throughout the world. Continuous messages from the angels are overlooked as coincidental, so often completely ignored.

The angel's voices have a much higher frequency than we are used to, making it difficult for us to hear them, therefore the angels use numbers as one of their forms of communication with us. Numbers form the structure of geometric pattern that exists in all living things, they are the building blocks of life itself. The angels identify us by numbers, that they use as if they are saying our names. They remind us that we are not on our own, by persistently allowing the same numbers, or sequence of numbers to be seen.

Maybe you look at the clock at the same time each day and have noticed that your birthday keeps appearing in minute form, even if you are busy and don't check the time often, you still see that same number somehow. A digital clock may have the same numbers in a different sequence, at different times of the day. If you pay attention to these clever coded messages, they will start to make sense to you. Notice that when you break a routine or habit, your, and as long as you stay focused you will have all the support that you need.

Angels have been known to appear during colourful dreams, or contemplative thought. Angels show their strength when they work with you, to guide you through the darkest times when unexplained events change the course of life itself. Angels are present quickly in emergency situations, with their calming forces evident in the energy of people and animals, who give endless strength and compassion.

You can become aware of the angels when you are spell-bound by nature and realise how important your place is within this world. Time is precious, a gift to be treasured. The angels with their hands on your shoulders remind you with love. "It's that time again, think about us."

The Tarot

There are twenty-two symbols used in the major arcana of the tarot, although there are twenty-four in this special edition which make this an important and treasured spiritual guide.

Each symbol represents a choice that is directly related to emotional balance. Including the influence of your family, friends and the community at large.

With this book you can learn how to expand your inner-vision, when a guide dog's senses take you on many incredible journeys, showing that the human viewpoint is only one of many.

Each sensory journey has a message. Look into each story closely and study what draws you into the scene. Watch to see if the story descriptions merge together, and try to detect hidden drama that is hiding away from you.

Pay special attention to how you feel. You will soon realise that your feelings are the most significant tool, for uncovering the information that you need.

Plan for the future, so that you can strive for the best possible outcome, just listen to your calm intuition and reasoning. If you change your mind, you will interpret the messages differently to reflect your choices.

Practice and enjoy yourself along the way, because these journeys are designed to stimulate your intuition until you can use your skills in every situation.

Choose an angel number between one and forty, then turn the page to your first journey. In a new diary, make a note of the number, and what it means to you.

Choose a maximum of three journeys a day. Your messages will remain clear if you stick to this rule. Each message will reflect your thought processes, so that you can move forwards with confidence. If you find that you keep choosing the same angel number, it means that you are ignoring an important situation that needs your attention. In this case, choose a new angel number to clarify what the situation is. As you explore in more detail, and allow time to pass, the answer will be uncovered, as you develop your intuition to guide you forwards.

Angel 1 of Passion

The angel of passion is number one, she refers to a passionate leader who is in tune with intuition and reasoning. You are a passionate leader that motivates others. Remember that love is always there for you. Passion is a driving force, a rocket-fuel for your ambitions. If you hold on tightly and persevere, your goals are much more likely to come into fruition. Use your imagination to practice how to use passion, especially in motivated arguments, your point of view will then be understood.

Passion needs restraint and the understanding of each one of us. As if harnessing a powerful tiger, then asking him to lead the way. Passion demonstrates serene harmony with the tiger that resides inside her soul. Stripped bare of restrictive ideals, her dark beauty reveals that she is the master of her emotions. If she allows passion to overwhelm her, she becomes a victim, then she is nothing. Yet the tiger within her personality is a tool of empowerment and infinite expression. The dancing movement runs through Passion, who invites you forwards, her naked hips swaying to a dance. As she asks you to continue your soul searching, she shines with the freedom of having absolutely nothing to hide. She must be fulfilled as a spiritual, earthly being as she demonstrates that you move forwards in a constant evolution.

A Passionate Intention

Inspired by a work of art at Peter Symond's College, Winchester. This is a very powerful visualisation to use when you are feeling uninspired and need to believe in yourself again. It asks you to create an emotional representation in images, on the subject of passion.

Imagine that you are back at college and have the use of an empty squash court, to explore your creativity. Your backpack, slung casually over one shoulder is fully equipped with used chalks, charcoal and paint. Your enthusiasm builds when you uncover your new work space, as you pull the creeping ivy away from the metal door, that has an empty hole, where once there was a handle to turn.

Your footsteps echo when you slowly step into the building, you feel as if the ghosts are brushing past you, whispering in your ear while leaving to hide in the dark corners, to watch your every move. You breathe in the taste of the past and take your first impression of a floor that is many shades of dirty grey. A faded and dusty emptiness with a sad breeze sits heavily on your shoulders.

This place aches for the life breath of white squeaking trainers and swinging squash rackets, held by competitive, determined young men wearing white tee shirts and shorts, that expose their naked legs that have been hiding under tight jeans, all winter long. You switch your thoughts away from the adolescent men while you stare up to the white sky, visible through gaping holes that are revealed by fallen tiles. The grey walls are a blank canvas for you to paint a masterpiece. This room positively calls to you, like a lost portal waiting to be opened with your magical energy.

With fierce ambition you begin to fasten wall paper to the cold, breeze block walls, securing the paper inside out, shoving painful push pins into the hard bricks with your sore thumbs while tearing off strips of oatmeal masking tape, as if it were your skin, until a large square area is covered completely.

The battered front door has been left open wide, to allow white sunlight to stream through. The brightness reveals the darting silhouette of a small tabby cat, with long white whiskers, that tickle as he stretches forwards, to lean his head into your legs. You stroke his velvet back, grateful for his company, as he purrs a happy song and leaves his warm, musky scent lingering on your hands. He examines your smudged watercolour paints delicately with his sensitive whiskers that fill your artistic fingers with a tingling rush of enthusiasm that prepares you to work.

Stepping back with a smile, you are able to imagine the picture you want to create. Time is of the essence as your breathing quickens, reminding your fingers to sketch the ideas, chasing them out of your thoughts and applying them onto blank paper. You lean against the wall, to lovingly touch and admire faces that are taking shape, whispering as they stretch and yawn, to become alive in the beautiful stillness of this place. Your Imagination creates all of your passionate dreams, right here and now.

You imagine the people that are involved with your hopes, until they seem to come alive as you draw. Their voices are clear and even their forms appear to be animated. Their clothes are designed in dramatic styles and swirling fabrics are dyed with strong colours.

There is one person that means a great deal to you, a valuable person that takes time to sketch very carefully, in the colours that represent their personality with bright eyes painted with feeling. The picture begins to open up now, as your characters make way for you to enter into their world.

Parting the way, they move over to give you the centre stage. You sketch yourself quickly and allow your hands to move freely and instinctively. You touch your face, to feel how your bone structure is like a living sculpture and your skin is supple, warm and glowing pink while moulding beautifully to your framework. Your cheek bones and jaw line shape you with three-dimensional form. Just as your hair is wildly alive, shiny and warm to the touch. Your hands express passion, so celebrate them. Your fingers are loose and free, so let them be strong.

You believe in yourself again, as you touch the picture and pick up the little cat, who is dipping his paws and long whiskers into your paint palette. He continues to purr as you hold him and put your face in his warm fur, to linger on his musky scent that smells like the warmth of sunshine.

The mischievous Devil

Passion is represented by the terrifying figure of the devil, in the major arcana of the tarot. While he adds an element of excitement, chase him away with all the energy you possess because he will not bring you peace. Keep your partner close to you with positive words. This is a loving relationship that must be kept in balance while you ensure that you both receive enough emotional fulfilment together.

With the fierce protection of a positive attitude. You will both establish the ultimate respect for each other. Keep that balance strong because you are attractive and may unknowingly be tempting superficial friendships that may not be helpful to you, or anyone else. Be aware of your actions and maintain your authority and poise always.

Take the next step

Choose a new angel number that reminds you of the kind of passion that helps you to find balance while you read the next sensory journey.

Angel 2 of Daydreams

The angel of daydreams is number two, she shows you that whatever your gender may be, exciting feminine and masculine energies can work together, to enhance a relationship with a heightened awareness. Angel number two is the symbol of unity between two individuals who continue a warm and trusting partnership.

This unity connects you as you watch your partner sitting beside you in the autumn sunshine. As you watch the energy around her body, you become more aware of her than ever before. Your mind's eye detects shades of yellow that surround her, while you share a closeness without speaking. In this precious moment, she allows your aura to communicate with hers. There is no boredom here, in this space where only peace exists. As if a bubble keeps every interfering thought away, for a few moments of this connection without words, there are none to say. They are meaningless as if time has become frozen.

The sacred rocks

Cave Hole on the Isle of Purbeck, is on your mind as you settle down to rest on your front while your therapist drapes your smooth hips with a warm, white bath sheet that gives you permission to close your eyes, in the velvet shadows of this small, quiet room.

Your therapist has a gentle smile, evident in the high notes of his voice as he whispers, "Allow your shoulders to relax and release all of their tension." The outline of his shoulders shows that they are loosely squared, to form a dominant silhouette that looms above you in the play of grey shadows, cast by three thick pillar candles. Their excitable flames dance and flicker when a gentle breeze of intrigue, gusts through the gap in an open window.

You are carried on a daydream to Cave Hole where your therapist asks you to. "Breathe in deeply to prepare yourself for a new day." "Think of the colour of morning sunshine, as the sun penetrates the energy aura that surrounds your body with its bright light." He continues the soft notes of his watercolour words that blend the colours of your aura, freely on to the open pages of your mind. He looks down at you then smooths his flat palms over the crescents of your eyelids. With a long sigh, he releases the words. "Breathe out slowly and imagine that you are releasing the sun's radiant shades of yellow from your lungs. Imagine the morning sun rise, as quiet roads stretch out in front of you. In the distance, a sea scape is shimmering. A unity feather floats down while morning birds sing and seagulls wail while a flock of geese fly south. The calm waves crash on to wet, shiny pebbles, that are pulled back by the force of powerful tides."

His energy feels reassuring while he supports you at this moment with his calm hands on your shoulders. His words fall on your ears in soft, low tones. "Just as you are, relaxed, comfortable and secure, close your eyes."

You fall into a dream where amazing shells whisper your name while a cave opens wide, to reveal a giant echo chamber, projecting up natural music to another world. Far away in the distance, you can hear his rumbling voice that blends with the vision of lucid, fluid underground water that shimmers with perfect light. A flock of seagull's cry while amazing shells continue to whisper your name.

He continues to resonate with you, as he asks you to "keep the busy pages of your mind calm and clear," as he takes you to the wild cliffs at Cave Hole, where he asks you to. "Lie down on the bed of soft grass that grows between the rocks." You hold on tightly, as you look down over the edge of the treacherously rugged cliffs that overlook Durlston Bay. You are supported by the grey, slabs of rock that form this ledge. The rocks hold chronicles of mystery, in between their layered ridges. As you run your hands over the smooth, textural stone the sacred strength of the rocks, connects your energy with the salty sea waves, that lick hungrily against the shore below. They sense your presence here, while your mind drifts around the vast expanse of sky that hangs above the ragged cliffs. You feel like she has been waiting for you to notice her. Now she silently watches your arms touch the horizon while they are stretched out widely, released again then stretched out until you are lifted out of your body, so that your soul is hovering above yourself. You look down on your resting body, with forgiving love and empathy that allows you to enjoy a pleasantly weightless sensation. You continue to float, as if you weigh no more than the lightest feather of all, and listen to the music of the ocean, pouring out of the speakers. In the stimulating tranquillity of this room, the ragged waves crash against the shore and pound against the pebbled sand over

and over again, shaping the coastline with every powerful
touch.

The hermit

The daydream is represented by the hermit, in the major
arcana of the tarot. He illuminates the way to wisdom and
enlightenment. Follow the white glare, of the old hermit's
mysterious lamp, let it show you a hopeful way forwards,
through the long dark nights filled with the thick fog of
doubtfulness. When the fog of worries clears, you will
knowingly see clearly, so that you can progress with a slower,
better path for a greater quality of wellbeing. Look at your
unique qualities and use them wisely then everything will fall
into place while you shine your light. Smile and be confident
because everything will be alright.

Take the next step

Wait for an angel number to find you. Use the next number that
you see or hear to take you to the next sensory journey to
explore.

Angel 3 of Friends

The angel of friends is number three, she is a friend who sees the beauty in your wide and expressive eyes, that look for the good in others and hopes that their lips speak only words of kindness. Angel number three stands beside you, she asks you to continue to walk with the knowledge that you are in good company.

Speak out loud while walking and don't worry. This firm chat with yourself, keeps order and balance of an otherwise chaotic mind. The result is that you are able to uncover what is really important now. You actually talk to yourself very often during the day. Understand that this is a good method to use to organise everything that you do. Speaking it is just expressing who you are, as if you are talking to a good friend. Be open to new ideas, as angel number three highlights a need for creativity. Your expressive voice must be heard, so speak out to the world when you are ready, or to those that you are closest to. Make yourself understood to those who want to listen.

The Bluebell Wood

A visualisation to show that there is always a friend nearby while you imagine that you are on holiday near the bluebell woods at Durweston, Dorset. Imagine that you have taken yourself off to explore the surrounding area. You are walking along a yellow, compacted mud path where tall hedgerows crackle with tiny mice, scurrying busily to gather berries, while the blackbird feeds the open mouths, of hungry chicks with pink wriggling worms.

You scramble over a rocky bank and find yourself enclosed in brambles that twist together to form a cage of prickly branches. A grey pigeon flaps his wings eagerly while he performs his mating ritual that sounds like the sails of a boat when the wind falls. He croons contentedly then pauses while a pheasant soars out of the undergrowth, startled by your presence here, he squawks in a noisy protest at being disturbed.

You slowly pull away the scratching, twisted brambles from your arms, until you are free to walk through the dense, green ferns that are open and alive with natural growth. As the silence speaks, you feel like it can hear your needs, nourishing your hunger for stillness and peace right now.

You are aware of everything as the silence listens to you. But your instincts do not alert you to a steep drop ahead and as you lose your footing, you reach out for creepers to hold, in the process you scrape your outstretched hands. You grab hold of tree roots, to stop your feet from slipping then the ground crumbles and the force of the tumbling earth takes you down.

Thick carpets of damp moss cushion the jutting out tree roots, until the bare earth exposes sharp flints that tear at your skin while you slide uncontrollably down the steep bank. When you are still, you breathe in deeply through your nose, trying to hold your breath for a count of four then breathe out powerfully and completely, totally releasing all of the air from your body.

You feel no pain, just helplessly floppy and loose limbed, absolutely weightless and at the mercy of anything while you enjoy this frozen moment.

Piecing together the scattered picture, you understand that the blue haze that surrounds you, is a sea of living bluebells. You sit up to pay attention to the mauve and blue mass of flowers that fills this staggeringly beautiful woodland. Then, suddenly drained of all energy, you sink heavily into the sea of bluebells that thrive underneath tall, towering tree branches that reach out like the arms of parents to carry life itself. Silent and strong, gently creaking to allow squirrels to run and jump from branch to branch.

As you lie heavily on your back in the silence, you survey the canopy of trees, and inhale the heady fragrance of bluebells and damp moss, filling your senses completely, helping you to relax into the moment.

You are disturbed rudely from your dreams by the bushes that move and rustle loudly. Turning towards the sound you prepare for your escape then see the magnificent silhouette of a stag that seems menacing, until you see his ornate antlers and recognise him as a friend.

He carries a statuesque presence and a calm authority as he freezes in a white haze, to listen to your breathing.

The stag listens to each and every breath. Somehow, he recognizes you as a friend and suddenly stops to glance at you briefly before he strides through the sea of cleansing bluebells and leaves behind a feeling of awe, a gift for you to remember forever, even to take with you into your dreamworld.

The guiding star

The bright star in the major arcana of the tarot, guides you like a very good friend, defining your mood with positive, expressive light. As a symbol of living love, the star reminds you to look at the attitude of others, be positive with your thoughts and pay attention to new learning opportunities that come your way, then you will be prepared to take on new, exciting responsibilities.

Take the next step

Think about your friendships and about how important they are to you. The first angel number that you think of now, is associated with your friends. Take the next step confidently while you turn to the next sensory journey, knowing that there is always a good friend right by your side.

Angel 4 of Release

The angel of release is number four, he shines an awakening blue and white light around you at this moment. This is to wake you up to the fact that, you must maintain a vital balance of all the earthly elements. You depend on a healthy environment.

Exercise your dynamic influence, to help sustain the harmony of all living things on this earth. Look to the animal kingdom for inspiration. Give yourself permission to enjoy all situations for what they are, without human judgement.

The living darkness

The ancient wisdom of Lucy Hill at Burley in the New Forest, are evident in the huge empowering stars that fill the large expanse of dark blue sky. This release invites you to explore an unforgiving, unknown forest path where you are open to the shrill, eerie shriek of hidden foxes, that hangs on the chill of your shallow breath.

Silence descends for the longest time, causing you to long for company as a strange sense of anticipation creeps across you. Your face sticks to clinging cobwebs that blow in the silky air. The awakening hoot of a male tawny owl breaks the stark silence, echoing through the ancient woodland with an eerie call, while the moonlight casts an icy blue glow between terrifying shapes of twisted trees that bear the image of distorted fingers, stretching out to touch you.

The soft moss on the ragged bark feels like an unfamiliar old man's beard. The trees above smile reassuringly while the tawny owl swoops towards you like a golden messenger, swiftly gliding past you to turn up the light of the stars.

You lean across a fallen tree who is a friend that welcomes you with a velvet carpet of moss. You gaze at the sky and interpret the stars and stark, blue moonlight in your open sketchbook, as astonishing insights fill your vivid mind.

Your imagination evokes an enchanting figure who has an ethereal, ghost like paleness. She has a petite silhouette and joyfully wavy, white hair that cascades all the way down her supple back. As you sketch, she becomes radiant underneath the light of the shadowy moon.

Universal life force energy is depicted in patterns with your pencils, as she connects with the different elements that exist in this world. As she allows the forests, oceans and all of the universe in its splendour to speak through her.

If she could grow wings she would fly and if she had a mermaid's tail, she would swim across the ocean. Even the ragged trees dance with freedom.

As moonlight illuminates her on the blue shadowed paper, you smudge, change and rub the edges of lines which capture her wild spirit. Defining her existence with subtle, expressive highlights. Your fingers slowly trace the contours of her face, until you close the humming book with thoughts of the beautiful, singing painting that your sketch will become.

Take the next step

Dreams become useful when you take notice of what they mean. Think about a dream that sticks in your mind. Try to understand what situation the dream is highlighting then choose a new angel number, use the sensory journey that it relates to as a tool to help you explore the meaning.

Angel 5 of Progress

The angel of progress is number five, she shines a fiery torch of positivity into your space. This angel asks you to look into a mirror that reflects back happy childhood memories. The precise eyes of your inner child can look closely at every detail of the beautiful outdoors, in a creative way that inspires everything to become alive in your hands. Bring the outdoors into your home and feel the refreshing difference when your home is inspired with natural materials.

Masterpiece of the Sun

As you walk past an ancient oak tree at Ringwood in the New Forest, it seems familiar to you. Your hands find tall, dense hedgerows that grow beside deep, damp ditches that you fall into. Your fingers discover that the edges support lush, green clover. You stop to listen to the sound of laughter, that scatters like happy music, casting spellbound shafts of light throughout a magical garden that does not seem to exist at all.

It is only a dream, that fades away when you awaken in the night, soon you fall in love with sleep again, until the darkness of your bedroom is filled with shafts of light that return you warmly to a dream where you visit the magical garden, to understand a butterfly's view of the world.

The emerging shapes are captivating, opening out slowly with a disciplined effort, stretching out a masterpiece, to dry its fresh paint in the warm yellow breaths of the sun, that breathe life into the curved, sculptured edges. Both armoured wings are of a similar size, although the difference of colours is very starkly evident, as the Holly Blue dries her wings evenly to reveal the palest glimmering tones, of soft porcelain blue, laced with black, embroidered edges. Her wings frame the earthy tones of her proud chest beautifully while the sun admires her efforts, as she watches every precious movement then retreats behind a scurrying cloud, to allow the wind to cool her creation.

A Tortoiseshell butterfly distorts her shape in flight with bedraggled copper tones and faded black antennae that crown her head with a warm, magnetic reassurance. She glances at the Holly Blue with exquisitely tuned, compound eyes. She carries a gentle calmness that encourages the Holly Blue to take her first flight.

As the breeze whispers encouragement, they rise together, to investigate the flashing movement of a Cabbage White, who's scent is his signature. They adore each other's' flight, waving their enchanted rhythm wildly to dance against the blue sky.

The swift movement of grey shadowed clouds, causes the sky to distort and darken, as the Holly Blue falls under the spell of jagged edges, that cut and scrape her bright colours away. Tight ropes cocoon her while vibrating eyes invade her space, in a threatening manner. She closes her wings together while she becomes perfectly still, as the silent sky turns grey, to signal that a hush is descending over the still garden.

Silently the butterfly speaks with colours to the vibrating eyes. The many shades of colour appear in shimmering waves of light that move in slow, pulsating motions with the palest hint of softness, that clouds her captors focus while bright orange and gold touches the depths of his soul.

The invisible time sweeps past with a feather-like touch that her captor feels in his conscience, causing his merciful fingers to raise the harsh net, to allow the flight of the butterfly, who stretches her wings widely, leaving the ground behind with a haze of rainbow light that merges into a wake behind her. Her magnificent antennae stand proudly like golden, enchanted wands of light while her compound eyes, view her surroundings as she absorbs the rays of sunshine.

The waiting Tortoiseshell joins the Holly Blue, she is enhanced with new brightness, as her tired colours glow with more transparent shades of copper and orange. While the mirrored angles of black define her beauty.

White blossom drapes mature apple trees, that change and shift their shape in a mesmerising pattern, as the butterflies move through the changing angles of their unique perspective that you find intriguing.

As a new day creeps through the gap in the curtains. The starkly bright daylight shines into your bedroom. As you begin to come round to reality, remember the colours of the Tortoiseshell butterfly, so that you can shine your new fresh and vibrant colours, in your aura today.

The teachings of the tower

Brand new ideas are represented by developing towers, in the major arcana of the tarot. These towers represent plans that are firmly supported, because they have a good structure If they are built into deep foundations. Sometimes one of the towers will fall representing new-developments.

If you are rebuilding your relationship, or starting over again with someone new. Build your tower on the best of intentions and the most fertile ground then dig deep enough foundations to support you both. Build a more stable relationship structure, even open up a world of inspiration that can be right at your fingertips.

Take the next step

Imagine a tower block built with toy wooden bricks, associate the tower with progress then count the number of blocks that are used. This is your new angel number; turn to this number to discover what message the next sensory journey has for you.

Angel 6 of Acceptance

The angel of acceptance is number six, he shows that it is time to nurture a new closeness with your family with open arms. This angel knows that you also have a desire to be surrounded by others in the community. You are well-balanced and naturally empathic which enables you to fulfil your caring role when you choose to be needed, you even feel confident enough to let others know that you need your own space. Accept the fact that life is a social affair, understand that your way of managing it is to be empathic with yourself and others in turn.

The call of a dolphin

Find freedom at Chesil Beach in Dorset. Imagine that you place the flat palms of your hands, firmly on a weather-beaten wooden sign post. Leaning against the post, you follow its guidance. With the definition of dark shade, leading you down an uneven, sandy path, loose stones push against your toes. The stones rub along by your side like companions as you walk. Until they are left behind on the narrow path that becomes an open beach.

As you observe with visual joy, the sea kissing the sky. They appear as one expanse of blended blue tones, forever changing. The depth of the ocean seems to surround you in a moving blanket of warmth.

The tide pulls your soul out to the horizon while your body stays fixed then slowly sinks into the suction of wet sand, as the hungry water laps around your splayed toes. You embrace the soothing, whispering waves that continue to lick your ankles, calming you with frothy splashes of foam. As if intrigued, the watchful winds have calmed.

You now have become part of this area of outstanding, natural beauty. Now you wait, in the serene humbling silence for nature to breathe in with you, then out again. Let your shoulders drop down as you exhale your breath, now imagine dolphins swimming towards you, through the churning, living oceans. Remember how the call of a dolphin, has a maternal quality to her sound vibration. That is reminiscent of a mother's primal instinctive calls, during the raw power of childbirth.

Resonate with the swirling pink and white colour frequencies that create kaleidoscopic patterns, as the dolphins swim into the bay, try to feel their vibrations moving through you. These vibrational frequencies cascade all the way down, to tingle the tips of your toes. Then up to your pelvis, even through your tight core muscles, pushing up again and flowing down your welcoming arms. Leaving through your fingers and the palms of your hands, to be felt as a tactile warmth. As you observe with visual joy, the sea kissing the sky they appear as colours that cascade to define a spiritual waterfall. A red heart pumps pure life with rhythmical pulsations. It glows in a mystical yellow haze, as if yet to be discovered. The shape of a winged guardian of light, with protective blue wings is highlighted through a transparent, white mist that hovers overhead.

Take the next step

Choose a new angel number, accept any relevant feelings that stand out for you this time. Keep these feelings while you enjoy exploring your next sensory journey with astonishing insight.

Angel 7 of Responsibility

The angel of responsibility is number seven, she is with you when you heave a sigh of relief that you made it on time, as you board the number seven bus, at seven o'clock in the morning on July the seventh.

Angel number seven will not be ignored, she encourages you to look for the truth in a matter that is playing on your mind. Most importantly, she reminds you to take your time to analyse the finer details of work projects. Although paperwork is not your greatest strength, it has to be completed, so reward yourself with plenty of free time later. If you really think about how many challenges each day brings, you will function more easily, if you can manage your days with a more relaxed mind.

Here are a few positive steps to practice, so that you can cope with all of your many responsibilities: Think about how you want to approach today. As you leave your bed, begin to wake up slowly. Allow yourself to grow into your body again with a refreshed outlook. Avoid looking in the mirror, save that for later, first feel who you are. Looking reveals the same face while feeling reveals your true-self. Awaken your energy centres by breathing deeply, take a minute to slowly balance and refresh yourself. You are blessed, stamp on the worry and the anxiety because they block your progress, they are irrelevant because you believe in yourself. Visualise yourself at the end of the day when you have achieved your targets.

Slow down to listen to your precious body, that is whispering that your back muscles are aching, even your energy needs to be refreshed. Just the act of leaving to change your space will make a dramatic improvement, so when you return feeling balanced, everyone else will benefit from your calming influence at last.

The bus of infinite possibilities

Imagine that you are waiting for the X12 bus to Dorchester in Dorset. It takes forever to arrive. So long, that boredom sets in. The creative ability of your subconscious mind, begins to imagine a bus stop, ancient and lost. The bus stop of infinite possibilities could be hidden by the overgrown hedge, that shelters the garden of a derelict house that holds mysteries, hidden behind dark windows. It's overgrown drive frames moss coated walls and the entrance, a sad grey porch coated with creeping vines, as nature takes over.

You hear a whooshing sound, so look over your shoulder. It feels like a gust of wind that seems to bring the bus with it. Strangely silent, it pulls over beside you at the deep curb. You step aboard this timeless bus. Timeless because it has no timetable then appears when you least expect it.

The patient bus driver waits for you to ask for a ticket. He has a deeply reassuring voice. You share a smile while he nods as you pass, to swap greetings with content passengers, who are all sitting closely together, wrapped up in warm coats while balancing wheeled cases, or clutching damp bags on their laps.

Younger people hang forwards with their headphones turned up to a high volume, and their long hair drooping into light screens of the latest mobile phones. Nike trainers are pushed against the moquette fabric of the seat in front, while pale jeans cling to endlessly long legs. Droplets of condensation gather in racing lines, then chase each other down, to form puddles at the bottom of steamed up windows.

The smell of used fish and chip wrappers that have been abandoned under the seats, blends with the earthy aroma of wet dog that lingers, in the atmosphere on this rainy day.

A frail elderly lady in the disabled seat wears a smart, cream mackintosh. She has layered it with a blue paisley scarf, just to keep out the cold, a red scarf around her head clashes oddly with the blue.

When the bus leaves, her trolley bag moves forwards. She reaches out to grab it, finding that her arthritic hands are painfully slow then her fragile blue knuckles fail to open. As she stoops to rescue the awkward wheel bag, you reach out and place the trolley in front of her, saving her balance just in time. She smiles, then you notice that her eyes shine through her lopsided glasses, as she mumbles a "thank you dear" while she shuffles backwards onto her seat.

You sit back again to relax and listen to the humming chatter of all the passengers that blends with the rumbling engine, until your attention is alerted to the bell. You watch the lady with the red head scarf, lean on her trolley to walk forwards.

You see a glimmer of youth as she moves then you see past the heavy leather shoes that reveal the most fragile of ankles. Her bowed legs in tan coloured tights once danced, but now barely support her frail body, as she slowly shuffles along the aisle to leave at the next stop.

You wonder who is waiting for her at home. You imagine that she lays the grimy table for two, then turns to touch her husband's coat that still hangs on the back of the kitchen door. The black and white television talks to itself, while she sits down on the well-worn ercol dining chair, opposite his, the cushion still dips from when he last sat down with her. The kitchen door creaks eerily and the smell of tobacco fills the room as if a pipe has been lit. She talks to him while she tries to make a thin ham sandwich and shakily pours tea into a porcelain cup, from a floral tea pot that leaks as she pours. Stacked up beside her, are dusty crossword puzzle books, and piles of yesterday's newspapers.

She stares vacantly at a photograph of her husband's smiling face, who's possession's surround her. She warms her hands against a small convector heater while watching him closely.

You wonder about this once radiant bride, even imagine that the man in the photograph is looking after her. She is taken in by his smile that seems to be fresh and new today. She affectionately remembers his hug, the smell of sweat on his working shirts and the softness of a beard, on his square chin. She feels his presence once more, as he welcomes her into the after-life with open arms.

As you blink then take a deep breath as the humming of the engine seems louder than usual. The gentle rocking motion makes you sit up to pay attention. Strangely you don't recognise the scenery, suddenly it dawns on you that the driver has taken the wrong turn. Right now, you are heading out into the countryside. Here you watch the passing fields, maybe dream that you are the only passenger on board, possibly in your dream this bus will take you wherever you need to go then you can visit whoever you want to see, in this beautiful time and space that is just for you.

Take the next step

The rain has cleared away with a breath of fresh air, as the bus arrives at your destination. Holding on to the grab rails, you feel your way along the rows of seats then leave refreshed and ready to start another sensory journey. Choose a new angel number to continue on your way.

Angel 8 of Forgiveness

The angel of forgiveness is number eight, she wears the figure of eight which is infinite with no beginning and no ending. A beautiful representation of true-love, even the eternal flow of life itself. Your continuous good intentions have been noticed, keep up the good work because the sun is shining on you. Give out those good vibrations then notice that they return to you in a steady flow of positive progress and well-deserved rewards.

The figure of eight

A figure of eight knot is symbolic of infinite love, it is also very important in sailing. This stopper knot won't slip at all, yet can be easily untied. Practice tying, then untying the figure of eight knot. While you tie it, secure the potential for achieving the limitless possibilities that love brings. When you pull the knot loose, release the ingrained habits that prevent you from progressing further with loving relationships.

This is how you tie the figure of eight: Take a shoe lace then tie a single eight with one end of the lace. Form a double eight, retrace the eight with the other end leaving a loop at the bottom. Finally pull all four strands of the shoe lace together, to secure the figure of eight knot.

The true love-knot

Escape to the solitude of Bryanston woods in Blandford Forum, Dorset. After running for miles, you decide to submit to exhaustion, so you lean back against the nearest tree. You can still hear his voice ringing in your ears as you look up into the blowing, whispering canopy of leaves of this old oak tree.

You slide to the ground, then retrieve the woven friendship bracelet from your pocket that was a gift from your true love. The frayed ends have fallen apart, so you tie them together, to form the shape of a single figure of eight knot then release them again. While you push your feet against the firm tree roots, you sorrowfully ask the ancient tree to share its energy with you. Your hands are placed over your chest, as if stuck, to feel your heart beating deeply. Now the forest breathes with you and listens, as you pull back tears until you are completely still.

As if on a rewinding film reel, your arguments play back in your mind. Firmly and with strong intentions, you ask them to "stop now." You make a fist, then punch the hard earth beneath you. Rubbing your sore knuckles, you gaze upwards and ask for help to forgive him because you really want to love him again.

Your imagination is a saving grace, it creates a waterfall of colours while you feel that you are sending the same image out to him. You tie the figure of eight knot again, to symbolise the loving union that you have, also want to keep hold of securely in your hands. They are surrounded with a glow of pearl white and sky-blue light that radiates from your forgiving and healing aura. Now you are in control, so you can begin your recovery with the help of the living trees.

Take the next step

Your forgiving nature is shaping your way. Put your best foot forwards, then choose your birth month for your next sensory journey, an angel number that the angels know and love.

Angel 9 of Humour

The angel of humour is number nine, he shows that a special compliment can be given as a light hearted approach, to break the ice with someone who may need a good friend. Use all of your heartfelt warmth, to enjoy being part of the local community today. Those unexpected meetings are a joy to share, reminisce on the past then bring some valuable memories back to life.

Bonfire night

The biting cold of a winter's evening, chills the silent countryside surrounding the Georgian town of Dorchester in Dorset, where your thick, woollen gloves remind you of your childhood. At this moment, you remember the intense heat, of a bright orange bonfire, gleaming in the charred stubble fields.

You think about the choking black smoke and remember popping, fizzing fireworks that draw you inwards, to watch closely as the bonfire burns bigger, bolder and brighter than you have ever seen before. You stand back quickly from the tremendous heat, startled by the black heart of the fire that has become alive. It smoulders fiercely, sounds like it snarls at you, while it devours all of the branches and worn-out chairs, that whine and moan "mercy," before they snap and break in the distorting heat.

Guy Fawkes grimaces menacingly from the smouldering pile, his eyes glow deeply to expose his orange soul, while his shredded trousers hang from a straw stuffed belly. A tingling temptation to feel sorry for him makes your stomach churn. To burn him seems to be a ritual that has gone too far, although your sympathy brings his invading spirit closer as you stare.

A sparkler fizzes in your gloved hand, distracting your attention while madly popping and spitting. Angrily you step away from Guy Fawkes, turning around to see lines of bright faces light up as your sparkler dramatically explodes, shooting out white, sparkling light that dances around your hand, until the dying embers fizz their last tiny sparks, before the stick becomes cold.

Your woollen hat is pulled down over your eyebrows, beautifully framing your shining eyes, it enhances your cheeks that burn with both cold and heat to the same intensity. You stare into the blazing fire which seems to lean towards you, burning steadily. The darting flames twist and leap against the back drop of a flat, black sky that is enhanced by live orange embers that pop, zing and crackle then fall to chill, totally extinguished by the cold hard earth.

A tall smiling lady passes round silver foil packages. You glimpse the white of the moon in her eyes, she has a mystical quality that smells like incense while you stare her mind pierces yours sharply, causing your ears to hum. She places a warm parcel into your open gloved hands. Caught in a trance, you watch her dark witchy silhouette drift away, as she turns her back to you then continues to hand out parcels to the crowd. You suddenly shudder violently, allowing the earth to absorb the energy she has left behind, pulling it all away from the core of you.

With a sigh of relief, you eagerly unwrap the hot parcel to find a potato that has been baked in the fire, sliced down the middle and filled with fresh butter. The first taste of crispy potato skin is hot, smoky and charred, although delicious with salty butter that melts in the warmth of your mouth. You all huddle together on this cold winter's night, to share sparklers that fizz and pop while you swirl them in the air. The sounds blend with magic and laughter as everyone stands together while jokes are told loudly by one, then shared on by others for all to hear.

Later that evening, after a warm bubble bath to wash away the powerful aroma of smoke. You roughly towel dry your hair then sprinkle sweet-smelling talcum powder between your toes. You wrap up in your mum's favourite, pink fleecy dressing gown then follow the humid, soapy scent of upstairs, along the cold, dark stair wall with your hand, where the witchy eyes that reflect the moon still follow you. The reassuring fragrance of homemade shortbread, lets you know that you are safely in the kitchen where you can relax.

Rosie is curled up in her warm basket, the yellow Labrador looks up at you sleepily to read your aura, she senses your fear and wags her tail slowly. Then stares down at your feet, watching the white trail from your talcum powder toes from beneath her dark eyelashes. Her knowing eyes water sleepily, as you run your fingers over her lashes, they look as if they are lined perfectly with black eyeliner, even the long, bristly whiskers around her mouth tickle your fingertips. You wonder if Rosie really needs those long whiskers, as you pull and tease them until she has had enough, so with a huge grumbling sigh, she sinks further into her large tartan blanket. The soft light in the dark, still kitchen gives the same tone of yellow that her pale fur radiates.

When you snuggle in beside her, all of the dark shadows dissolve to be replaced by a honey glow, that smells like sleep. A warm scent that you associate with comfort and love. Although she is clearly not impressed about being disturbed late in the evening, which her expression shows while she curls up even more tightly. A problem that you endeavour to sort out, by lifting Rosie's spirits until her tail wags more enthusiastically, because she has your full attention to play. Her scent changes as her mood lifts to become sweet and warming, as you push your face into Rosie's soft fur. She feels that you appreciate her, she needs this kind of simple reassurance from you every day. As you listen to her shallow breathing, you wonder what she is thinking, you connect with Rosie on her level, then open a path of mutual understanding between you.

Take the next step

Share your stories with humour today then tomorrow, do it all over again. Smile as you choose a new angel number, then turn to discover your next sensory journey.

Angel 10 of Appreciation

The angel of appreciation is number ten, he will not be ignored as he points out that sometimes your very best is just to take time out to rest. Focus on what you want to achieve. Keep an organised mind and routine, until you are ready to spring back into action then you can really go for it once more.

Lost at the nature reserve

A guide dog's senses take you to a wonderful area to run free, at The Milldown nature reserve in Blandford Forum, Dorset. The Milldown is a beautiful landscape of rolling hills, that contains managed areas of woodland and chalk grassland. Home to many varieties of butterflies and moths. This popular area, also provides a natural habitat that is essential for a wealth of wild flowers and birds.

This ideal area is much visited by dogs and owners of all descriptions, it makes a fantastic play and meet space for hard working guide and assistance dogs, that need to let off steam.

"My name is Stella I am a beautiful yellow Labrador guide dog and I am in charge at my family home." I look out for everyone, from the top of the stairs. From this position, I can hear the boys playing in their rooms, also watch the front door all at the same time. I am in my alert position because mum is up to something, so I stay poised, in a motionless front crawl with ears pricked up to listen while my body is perfectly still, so that I don't miss anything at all.

Tiger Lily licks her white paws, while sitting on the stair below me, she smooths her long whiskers straight, even though they bounce back to curl under again. The petite tortoiseshell cat fluffs out her silky fur, then sweeps her feather duster tail across my face, while casually stretching her body tightly in front of me. My warning grumble doesn't deter her at all. She can see that my eyes are sharpened to work mode, so she is amused when my ears twitch as she paws them to tease me, trying to distract me because she knows that I am poised perfectly still to listen.

"There it is." The chink of metal rings on the well-worn leather lead, against the soft, white leather of my working harness. I scramble down the stairs straight away, using my special speedy front crawl. At the bottom I pant, "here I am mum."

If I stand across the door, mum won't forget to go out today. I nudge her white trainers with my sensitive pink nose, because she has lost them again. Mum beams a smile of approval at me, then rewards me with a biscuit. I nudge her cream, belted coat with my nose that shows her where it is then I stand very still to wait. Sweeping her dark hair out of her eyes, mum takes this calm moment to slip the working harness over my head then buckles it securely around my slim waist. I wait quietly while she listens to the front door click closed behind her. I guide her hand down the garden path that is edged with large, round terracotta pots that are filled with a variety of fragrant herbs, including White Sage, Rosemary and French Lavender.

I stop to sit in anticipation at the end of the path. This is the very first curb on our tidy housing estate, the important starting point of our journey.

I watch the movement of mum's lips eagerly for directions, as Tiger Lily brushes against her ankles, I look left persuasively, hoping that mum understands that I want to take her to the Milldown today. She smiles while she speaks the command "left." My head moves so quickly, that mum swivels on the spot, narrowly missing a lamp post. I know that I am pulling to get to the Milldown, maybe just a little too tightly, so she tugs me back. I pant heavily with the sheer effort of our struggle, until my front paws seem to move on their own, scuffing along the well-worn pavement. I guide mum around tall, green wheelie bins, then sniff the stale beer that clings to green bottles that are piled up in battered recycling boxes. I guide mum around the obstacles of over grown bushes, so that she is not hit by the sticking out branches.

At the end of the street, I glance at her with guilty eyes, waiting for confirmation that I need to sit at the curb. She shows me her tight-lipped look, asks me to "sit," then carefully she reaches down to check that I have a straight back and even that my bottom is perfectly seated then she gives the command "forwards."

I stare across at a bright young Spaniel, who is walking a gentleman on the industrial side of the busy, main road. Tempted by the dog's energy, his earthy odour and style, I speed up to take a sniff while I draw mum's attention away from our usual route. I am unlikely to get away with this distraction technique, but it is always worth a try. Mum asks me to turn right towards the supermarket, she explains that we have to walk straight on. Feeling sad I lower my head, suddenly aware of my belt hook chinking against the metal ringed lead. I notice that the Spaniel has taken his dad down the narrow passage way between the tall, chain linked fences that guard grey, forbidding industrial units. Convinced that he looked at me, I raise my head high then sniff the air to catch his earthy scent, I begin a deep and rasping pant while thinking that maybe we can catch up with him.

We approach "the Milldown" along a woodland path with my heightened senses aware of the most interesting musky scents of dogs and the sharper, more pungent aroma of exciting fox trails. I begin to drool in anticipation then nudge mum's knee with my highly activated pink nose. This means "can I smile at people who approach us," mum just gives me a long stare that tells me that I must ignore all others when I am working. Mum pulls white tissues out of her pocket, to wipe long strings of drool away from my open mouth. She is so concerned about small matters, she even asks me to calm down, so I shake wildly to release all of my built-up tension.

Our special launching point is where the trees open out into the bright sunshine. Here, mum stands still and silently waits to have my full attention. I watch keenly as she asks me to sit quietly then wait as if frozen, for the moment when she slowly, but deliberately moves her hand up to her lips then enthusiastically blows the loud, shrill whistle three times.

"Off I go," with the high, clear sounding bell on my collar that let's everyone know that I am on my way. The chase is the best feeling in the world, so I don't hang about when there is new territory to explore. I dash off eagerly to introduce myself to a dog that appears to be right on the ridge of the hill. I run as fast as the speed of light with my bell jangling, then slow down politely as I approach. We work out our ranking with an upright dance, followed by a gentle whine, as a sensible greeting for this elderly Alsatian. I check who he is with a friendly bottom sniff then he finds my scent and suddenly becomes agitated. He wants me to back off, his warning is the loudest grumble of all. I get the message quickly then run away with my head low and tail well down.

Mums whistle calls me, I respond straight away and her open hand rewards me with a biscuit, her warm fingers touch my face to tell me that she is impressed that I have returned. "I will be back for more biscuits soon."

She will see me again when I have found the fox pooh. Please understand that my nose twitches uncontrollably to catch this strong odour that is irresistible to dogs. The breeze blows freely, so that the scent runs in waves through the thick grass. With my nose straight down to the ground, it becomes incredibly sensitive, working together with my tail that is tall and stands high in the air to balance my stance, it shows that I am on a mission. Discovering my trophy in the gorse and ferns, I roll around on my back in absolute joy. Just to make sure, I keep on rolling to cover my beautiful blonde coat in the smelliest, stickiest, black pooh you could ever imagine. It will be an absolute delight to show off my new fragrance to the other dogs now.

They call for my attention much more than mum's annoying whistle, so I mark my scent on a big clump of earth that smells like rabbit trails. This area is laced with tasty droppings, so my nose twitches madly, it points straight down to the ground again, as I walk in zig zag patterns to smell their paths and wish that the timid rabbits would venture out of their deep, dark underground burrows to play a game of chase with me.

An orange rubber ball suddenly skims past my nose, I jump to react, completely forget about the whistle then eagerly make chase. While in hot pursuit of the ball, I become aware of three, black Labrador dogs running along beside me very quickly indeed. A large dominant male takes the lead in front, a smaller slim female chases her chunky younger brother, who runs next to her. Their paws thud along the ground like horses competing on a race track. They are terribly fast, but I believe that I can catch up with these super fit dogs then the orange ball will be mine.

The dogs disappear suddenly, so I stand very still to wait for any sounds that tell me where they might be. I look past the blowing trees to the gravel car park where I pick up their scent again, so I walk forwards to watch them jump into the boot of a muddy Range Rover. The inside smells like unwashed dog blankets and tasty hide bones. I love this combination and want to introduce myself, especially as the largest dog carries the orange ball proudly in his mouth, while drooling and dribbling in a dominant fashion. Although their noses are sniffing the air to smell my rather strong odour, I still feel the need to let them hear a soft whine to say that I am here.

Suddenly a large hand grabs my collar, taking me by surprise and filling me with fear. Tucking my tail between my legs, I stay quiet and shiver nervously, even though I can hear mum's whistle. The man doesn't understand that I can find her on my own, so I whine loudly to say "please let me go." When he refuses, I pull as hard as I can while he grumbles crossly because he finds it difficult to hold me.

Panic stricken, mum tries to find me, she shields her eyes under the shade of the trees and she calls out for me over and over again. I can smell from this distance that she is worried and scared, all at the same time. She lets out a shout of delight, as she welcomes with open arms, a rather smelly, bedraggled yellow Labrador who is panting like a steam train. Mum feels the guide dog's badge to check that it is definitely me, because I am almost unrecognisable, even to her.

She hooks my lead on securely while the man explains in his Dorset accent. "I heard you calling and whistling, so I assumed this was your dog. She ran off with my dogs to chase a ball, so I thought I'd better hold on to her then she took me straight to you."

Mum thanks the gentleman for the trouble he has taken. She checks me over with her hands to see if I am injured, discovering with a sigh of relief that I am absolutely fine. Even though she says I smell terrible, I still have to work, so she lifts my working harness over my head while she mentions that I will have a warm shower when we get home.

Mum is still proud of me, even though I have let her down badly, by not returning to her whistle. She appreciates everything that I do for her, even though I am tired, I will still take mum home and after my shower, I can curl up tightly in my warm, comfortable bed.

Take the next step

Keep appreciation close to your heart, as you choose a new angel number then turn to your next sensory journey.

Angel 11 of Communication

The angel of communication is number eleven, he highlights the numbers one and one, which together are the components of angel number eleven and represent the very powerful, loving union between two people.

Two people who live together as twin souls with the willingness to walk side by side. Communicating in a way that heals, not in a way that wounds.

Everything has a voice

Listen to the voice of St Catherine's hill, Winchester in Hampshire. An iron age hill fort that calls to be visited as it lies still like a sleeping giant, on the horizon of the water meadows beside the river Itchen. The ground speaks of optimism for a productive year ahead, as you fall into a pattern of footsteps followed by many, on a well-worn mud path. You are blown away by the abundance of orchids and butterflies that flourish on these chalk downlands.

This may be the most important day of your life, that is how you feel, as your sandalled feet are brushed by the long grass. The shady hedgerows open out to reveal your deep intake of breath then your body relaxes enough to sit down to rest. While you absorb the expanse that lies before you,

You listen to the humming aeroplane that has escaped into blissful flight while the school playground is alive with the sound of shrieks and laughter. Cars stop and start like dinosaurs, rumbling past the manicured school field.

Now that you are away from all distractions. You breathe the fresh, clean air and hold it for seven seconds. When you release, you benefit from pushing all of the air out of your body then with a deep breath in you feel wonderful. You remove your sandals and start to walk down the wooden steps now. You can breathe so easily, more so than ever before.

You feel carefree, young and full of vitality as you stop still, to take a massive deep breath in then shout out, "ah," as loudly as you can, using the full power of your voice. Your feeble cry develops into a mighty roar, as if you are a lion, taking control again and again, to release all your tension completely. Having expressed your fears and anger to the world, you feel as if you have made peace with yourself at last.

Relief takes over like feathers from heaven, bringing tears to your eyes. You balance on each warm, wooden step easily, wiping your face and sniffing back fresh tears. You notice for the first time that each step is a different size and leads you closer to the busy community, that now seems to be pristine and new. In your awakened eyes, it shines so very brightly.

You are overshadowed by a copse of magnificent trees, as you tread on the final step where the bird song is vital communication while the dusty grassland that surrounds you, is alive with the wise crickets vibrating beat.

The school bell clangs, heralding the end of lunch hour and your accurate hearing detects the tones of each child's voice, as they line up in rows. You hear the cars hum to stop and start as the pelican crossing bleeps. You feel ready to go out into the community, like a child in the school playground, you are eager to explore and learn with confidence again.

Justice speaks out

Justice, in the major arcana of the tarot, reminds you to trust your family and work colleagues to hear you, even though communication may be slow at times, it often happens more successfully when you are not pushing for an answer.

Justice represents communication, so prepare to meet new people that help you develop your social skills. Strengthen your communication methods to attract the people that you want to be present in your life now. Work with empathic understanding of your partnerships, social groups and teams so that you can be completely aware of each situation, enabling you to treat each person with the attention that they need.

Take the next step

Imagine that a white feather lands on a number of your choice. The feather is a signal that your message has been received. Turn to that angel number with the confidence that there is an answer waiting for you in the next sensory journey.

Angel 12 of Boundaries

The angel of boundaries is number twelve, he smiles encouragingly at you while he helps to push away boundaries that block your progress, yet he still reminds you to protect yourself.

Some memories keep popping up when you want to progress with your future. When they rudely make an appearance in your mind, imagine that they are surrounded by a giant, clear bubble.

Package them neatly away inside the bubble then give the bubble a name while you blow it far away with the memories captured inside. If the memories float back to you, surround them in a bubble with a tougher skin than before and call it by the same name. Blow it away with much more effort than before, but remember that you are in control and will always win over these memories, so don't call them back to you again.

The healing process begins when you understand that you can manage your life, even thrive. Therefore, the bubble visualisation, is ideal for you to use to protect your personal energy field. Your imaginary bubble can be any colour that you choose, although the brighter colours bring much more positive results.

Surround yourself in your very best bubble as you enter a crowd of people their auras are all mixed up together, to form one collective energy, working in an unspoken communication. Without boundaries, an incoherent muddle of moving colours merges with no focus at all. With the boundaries of a bubble and space between each person, your aura can shine its unique colours with no interference from another and works much more efficiently, preventing mental and physical fatigue because of the continuous flow of positive energy to your body.

The community at the river

South bridge frames the busy river Frome that is alive with swimmers racing to touch the river banks while dodging small rowing boats and canoes. The picturesque town of Wareham benefits from this lively river community.

As you imagine that you are standing on the road, away from moving traffic, you touch the warm stone of the indented resting place, on the old bridge while you listen because you want to be aware of everything.

Away from the car fumes, the smell of damp earth leads to a picnic area, sheltered by trees that open out to reveal a footpath. You follow the sunny opening, while your face is brushed by weeping willows, as you are surprised by a friendly white terrier, who touches your hand with his inquisitive wet nose.

The tall bull rushes and reeds parade sharp edges like swords of defence that stand tall, swaying their large, rich brown seed heads against the delicate white flowers of the giant hogweed. The dense marshland grass parts to give glimpses of white boats that sway as the water churns noisily while larger boats pass by, sailing in from Poole quay to showcase their white sails raised tight and proud.

The clinking of wine glasses carries a sense of euphoria. A positive vibration that resonates through everyone here. Walker's exchange cheery greetings as they make space for you to pass by.

At the bridge, the river side benches are popular with hungry families who are tempted by the warm fish and chips smell, wafting towards them. Children sit together, swinging their legs while they balance white paper bags, full to the brim and spilling over with fat chipped potatoes, seasoned with salt and vinegar. They stab the hot chips with wooden forks, some fall onto their pale, bare legs and are then taken swiftly by sharp-eyed seagulls, scavengers who soar around the riverside, wailing and chuckling while they strut their dance on the waterside moorings.

Suddenly you hear a loud splash that creates rippling waves, so you pause to watch a confident, teenage boy swim to the shore. His head emerges from the water with a cocky enthusiasm, as he parades his bare chest proudly. In the stunned silence, you hear a youth yell "come on, you can do it," as a younger boy stands on the bridge wall, ready to jump into the deep river.

His mother encourages him, by forcing a smile while she shows off her blue bathing suit and white rubber cap, she strikes an elegant pose against the wall, before she jumps confidently from the bridge into the river, feet first.

Then the crowd's attention is fixed on him alone. Everyone can see that he is frozen to the spot on the edge of the bridge. They cheer him on, but he feels like he is letting the crowd down, so bows his head low. His mum jumps from the bridge again, and hits the water with a resonating "splash," while the crowd claps enthusiastically.

His two older brothers continue to take it in turns to jump, encouraging him as they do so. They seem to be oblivious to their younger brother's feelings, who's poor teeth are clenched together with such force that his jaw aches. They have not said anything reassuring to him, even though they can see that his fists are closed with tight knuckles while his wide eyes are pools of fear. Although they pay attention and stare, thinking of words to tease him with, when he drops his shoulders and steps down, defeated but realising his boundaries at last with a huge sigh of relief.

Take the next step

Think about the many colours and rhythms that you express with your energy. Let this influence the angel number that you choose while you turn to your next sensory journey.

Angel 13 of Sisters

The angel of sisters is number thirteen, she expresses her wisdom by encouraging you to keep a strong sense of direction. She is with you to keep you on the right path because a difference in circumstances, can change the direction of your life. Guidance is called for when you lose your way, it is not always possible to guide yourself and the sooner you realise this, the easier your life will become.

The thirteenth hour is not in our usual twenty-four-hour clock, even though it could be said that there are times during the day, when the ticking of the clock fades away into the background. To the dreamer, time has no relevance at all, yet their dreamscape may be so realistic that it feels like reality. Time moves on in the conscious awareness of all of us, but our subconscious minds do not need its boundaries, therefore allowing us to take a rest, so that we can achieve our full potential during our waking hours.

A birthday reunion

Inspired by Bournemouth Train Station, Bournemouth in Dorset. A train journey to remember with an emotional reunion. "Welcome to Bournemouth train station" the station master shouts over the intercom. "This train is for Christchurch, New Milton, Brockenhurst and Southampton Central."

You are caught in the surging crowd that scatters in all directions, signalling the trains arrival. Wheel bags and heeled shoes push past, as your lowered gaze notices scruffy work jeans, white sports shoes, high visibility jackets and stooped heads. Some wearing printed fabric face masks while others disposable blue surgical versions that cover their unaware expressions, as they long for their next cup of coffee, at the nearest café.

You find a quiet window seat, right at the back of the busy carriage then as the train moves forwards, you sigh with relief while you clutch a shoe box that is wrapped in blue foil and dressed with a silver ribbon. It is your sister's birthday and you are going to visit her. It has been such a long time since you have seen her, but now the coronavirus restrictions are lifting, you are happy to travel again.

The swaying rhythm is soothing while the window frames the ever-shifting scenery. Just at this moment, the train slows enough for you to glimpse through the trees to a garden that displays its washing line of pristine, white towels and all in one baby suits that remind you of the smell of fresh talcum powder. Tiny socks line up proudly next to the pale blue vests that are secured with mum's best wooden clothes pegs; you can tell that every one of them has been fastened with love. Dad's white shirts and blue jeans, bow at the knees as if he has just stepped out of them. They perform their dance of freedom while swaying on the washing line, caught up in a gust of wind so that the legs dance comically.

The train window frames the rushing by images of many similar shaded, paving slab back yards that house tall, blue wheelie bins. Damp slime clings to dark mossy corners that thrive with new growth while brave bind weed climbs up dripping gutter pipes. You watch and listen, as a soothing voice broadcasts over the tannoy, "the next stop is Branksome." As you approach, the train slows to a stop then the doors open wide.

A lady with ruffled blonde hair finds a seat next to you, she has been rushing, consequently she struggles to catch her breath. You admire her black trousers and blue denim shirt that hugs a slim, youthful figure and her printed, polka dot face mask reveals smiling, busy eyes. She comments on the pretty bow on the box that you are holding.

She begins to describe the large, fancy dresses that she used to sell, in a voice that is full of expression. You are captivated by her enthusiasm and hang onto her every word. She explains that her name is Sally then after casual chat about the weather, she begins to tell you more about the most beautiful dress shop in an exclusive area of London. "Ladies would come in to see me for a personal fitting, now we don't even try on clothes before we buy them. Back then, we altered dresses to fit someone perfectly, we even knew each lady's size, so when a new dress arrived, I phoned straight away to ask them to come and try it on. We had all the best designs in all colours and such elegant evening gowns."

You imagine the glamorous, colourful shop, filled with the excitement of the customers who received so much enjoyment from the attention of this lady. How they felt like new, beautiful women because the dress would always fit perfectly. Although sometimes too expensive and then they would wait for it to be reduced in price.

Sally continued to describe how she spotted one of her customers walking past her shop. Knowing that her dress had dropped in price, Sally chased her all the way down the street. A trailing silk ball gown on a hanger, lifted up high with one hand while waving the other and shouting out, "it's reduced, it's reduced!"

"One day the door opened widely and Princess Anne marched in, absolutely covered in mud from horse riding. She stood in the changing room and pulled off her jodhpurs, leaving them crumpled on the floor. The Princess said briskly," "hurry up, I need a dress!" "She waited to be fitted for a new dress to wear straight away." The Princess was usually pleased with her outfits, she was always concerned that her appearance had to be perfect, even though she was in a hurry to get to her next engagement. It was a pleasure to make her look stunning and to meet her requirements was a great privilege."

Sally's voice slows, to tell you that she misses her job and explains that It's all online shopping now, so sadly her business closed down. The train slows gradually, to stop at Southampton Central, so you wish Sally well, as you bravely mind the gap and leave the train behind.

As you step out, your thoughts lead you to compare the train ride to a life journey. You realise that some people stay on the train until the end of the line while others leave at different stations to continue on their way without you. You find it intriguing to think that everyone you meet, has a reason for being on the same path as you, even if they just pass you by.

You find it hard to cope with the stark, dazzling brightness of the sun that reflects off the platform. You ignore the shoulders that knock into your arms while you are caught up in the crushing surge of people that make no sense to you at all. They are indistinguishable in the light. You catch a glimpse of the ticket office and the bright confectionary kiosk. This landmark means that you are heading in the right direction, so you slow down, to welcome a surge of relief. To be able to walk freely, out in the open is exhilarating.

The young woman standing at the sandwich bar moves towards you. Lost in between barriers and people, you push through to greet her with arms outstretched. You give your sister the blue foil wrapped box, tied with a silver ribbon. She opens it in delight and pulls out a doll that you have chosen for her. You can see on her face that she remembers that as a child, she played with hers until the hair was falling out and the clothes were lost. This princess doll is identical in every way, except that it is yet to be loved.

She holds the doll, adorned with a sparkling gown and displays a delighted smile, that shows her magical, child-like quality once again. Suddenly there is a break in the crowd and comparative silence brings relief. You think that the continuous movement of people with plenty of directions to choose from, may cross paths with you again and then you may benefit each other when you slow down to talk. Even family and friends can pass by if you allow them to. Any man, woman or animal has a reason for being on the same path as yourself, even if they just pass you by.

Temperance and discipline

Temperance means moderation in the major arcana of the tarot. A gentle reminder to freely give the very best of yourself to your partner and children. Work hard to stay in touch with friends, participate in groups of interest that are vitally important for personal and social growth, respect that you are only human, temperance asks you to keep everything in balance and take time to rest. Temperance is represented by the strength of sisterhood in the tarot. With a message to be admired and respected, because she is the mother of all.

Take the next step

Close your eyes then imagine you are underneath a roof of sweet, scented apple trees that are bursting with ripe fruit. Choose an angel number for your new sensory journey, while your sister is on your mind, the next journey will be about her.

Angel 14 of Choice

The angel of choice is number fourteen, he stands in the centre of a crossroads to show you that there is a decision to make, you must choose to continue to work hard in the same direction, or turn back to an easier route. Remember to choose what you love to do, not what you struggle with, because you must be true to yourself. Listen to your inner voice to clarify this decision. Your journey today is designed to let you grasp what is really important now.

A natural foot-bath

As you approach the breath-taking surroundings of Kimmeridge Bay on the Isle of Purbeck, the steep and uneven stone steps lead down to a wooden slatted bridge, that takes you over the estuary and down still further to the rocky beach. You steady your balance, take one step at a time then drop down onto the opening of light, flooding towards you. Your eyes widen, to notice the contrast of starkly bright light against the stunning, dark layers of Kimmeridge clay.

The scent of damp seaweed that clings to the rocks is refreshing while the force of powerful tides that are ruled by awesome waves, recklessly smash their magnificent shapes into pieces, shooting spray that surges back against the clay ledges. These towering cliffs are formed with fossils, preserved in shaped layers of the jagged cliff face. The occasional rock becomes loose enough to drop down onto the beach with a resounding "crash" like the drums in a rich orchestra of natural music. You immerse yourself in the sounds and sink down onto the smooth rocks of a clear marine pool then touch the carpet of damp, puffed sea weed, decorated with bubbles that burst under foot. You sink down again, absorbing the deep yellow rays of afternoon sun. Tension is shed as the cleansing water carries it away. You cup the salt water in your hands, feeling it trickle through your open fingers, like liquid gold, while the sun makes rainbows as the golden droplets fall. All the time, the powerful tide echoes and pushes against the jutting out cliffs that silently enclose you. The water gently laps and circles you, becoming deeper. Your rock pool has a violet blue haze and the warm, golden tones shine through the ambient light, as you follow the tactile clues all around you, like the floating seaweed brushing against your ankles. You touch the lines on a rough limpet shell and run your forefinger around the circular ridges of an ammonite.

You push down into the soft, sinking sand under your feet and feel secure as your other senses take charge. While the powerful tide echoes and pushes against the jutting out cliffs that silently enclose you.

The wheel of fortune

The wheel of fortune in the major arcana of the tarot, is depicted here, by a deep red rose that radiates bright colours that turn in the motion of a wheel. The living rose represents your appeal to others. Keep on planning ahead because the rose petals are fragile and can fall if neglected. The beautiful rose is only in bloom for a short time, so make the most of the summer sun, find all of your skills to gather new-opportunities. While you are doing so, you may be surprised to find that there are financial or material rewards, even the rewards that friendship brings. Check your phone for missed calls, look at your expenditure then compare it to your income. Your bank account is not just there for you to survive, make enough money available for you to really feel comfortable. You choose your own path with the wheel of fortune, so keep your ideas in perpetual motion, as the influences around you are clearly making a positive difference each day.

Take the next step

The wheel of fortune is constantly opening up new-opportunities for you. Focus on a new angel number, as the wheel turns to take you through to your next sensory journey.

Angel 15 of Self-Worth

The angel of self-worth is number fifteen, she holds her amethyst staff to remind you, that just because someone else loves you, doesn't rescue you from the project of loving yourself.

Listen to your gut feeling, for answers that you just can't find anywhere else. Interpret any confusion that gets you down, into feelings rather than words. Make a plan to listen to yourself first, then you can successfully listen to the people that you love.

The long white cane

The Georgian market town of Blandford Forum in Dorset, sets the scene for this sensory journey, where the long cane demonstrates self-worth.

In this challenging journey, you may imagine that you are using the long-cane to find your way. Think about how this would feel, and when you are ready, put on a pair of the darkest blackout glasses, that only allow you a limited amount of vision, and continue the journey.

As you walk, every dip in the pavement becomes familiar, as the ball tipped cane hits against the tall red brick walls of town houses. Some in old, weathered stone that home lichens in several rough textures and deepening shades of grey. The walls themselves cast dark shadows of interest, appearing as solid objects to walk around. The shadows startle you, as they jump out of nowhere, taking on awkward shapes, starkly silhouetted against white paving stones.

Georgian window sills stand out, to show off their proud depth and structure. Dark window panes frame sleeping cats, and window sills that are decorated with dead flies, and hanging ornaments. Some homes are shops that have kept their characterful Georgian appeal. As your cane finds a pale blue door, with glass window panes.

The dark shade makes you duck your head to enter. You feel your way with the cane, and it shows you the footprints of many people, well-worn into the centre of stone steps that lead down into the shop.

You become aware of the temperature cooling dramatically, and your eyes begin to adjust to the darkness. As your heart beat calms, the scent of many varieties of flowers tells you that you are in the florist. The ancient wooden beams add to the floral symphony, improving the delicate tones, and enriching the sweetness with a musty depth. Your weight causes complaining floorboards to creak, and the door decides it's had enough of watching you, and closes while ringing a brass bell to alert all, of your presence.

While sweeping her short, auburn hair out of her face, the florist asks if she can help. "Can I have a look please?" you reply. She looks down at you, finishes her mug of cold coffee, then says, "yes, just call me when you need me." She shuffles out of sight but leaves behind, her watchful gaze.

You can imagine that mice play here at night, and that maybe the beautiful, hand-crafted wicker baskets of sweet peas, hide a few holes. Every evening, when the florist fights with the door that jams shut, and turns the key in the ancient lock, large, brown town-mice emerge from hidden cavities, to run between the yellow geraniums and metal buckets of pink and white carnations.

The mice play around sunflowers, that are star of the show, as you walk between tall stemmed pink roses, and fancy lilac hydrangeas. You choose to ignore the worrying image of giant hairy rats, and keep mice on your mind, while you pick out a bunch of bright sunflowers for your friend, then notice dried bunches of statice in all colours, hanging from large, heavy oak beams. Recycled jars, tied with bright ribbons, are placed on high shelves, in the company of intricate cobwebs, that catch flies for extremely large spiders, that watch and wait in the dustiest of corners.

You can feel the florist watching you impatiently, so you hand her the sunflowers. At a glance you see her straightening the creased white apron, that she wears over tight jeans, and a short blue shirt. She covers her mouth as she yawns, and grabs the ball-point pen that is rolling out of her reach. You want her to "wake up," but the lady continues her lethargic attitude while she coughs into her hand, and mumbles that she is happy to send the flowers, then she bends over, leaving her lower back exposed, and hits her head with a loud "thud" on the jutting out table top, of her ancient work desk. While rubbing her bruised forehead, she takes your friend's address and your payment, then opens a large, traditional cash register, that rattles with loose coins as the draw opens, and slides closed with a "ping" of the bell, and a rhythmical "whirr," while the receipt is printed out and placed into your open hand.

After wrestling with the brass handle of the pale blue door, you find yourself in the bright dazzle of day light. Frozen to the spot in confusion, the heat is overwhelming. You begin to walk with no idea of your surroundings at all. Although today, walking with a long-cane, while you listen for a break in the traffic, feels like being detached from everybody else. Your awareness has to be on every sound and movement, not on yourself. You must be focused completely. Yet in this moment, you step forwards, and walk straight into a car that is badly parked, right across the narrow pavement.

Feeling confused, the painful dazzle of sun light slows you down. You feel with the cane, to steer you around the car which takes time, and puts you in the dangerous situation of being in the path of on-coming traffic.

Completely distracted from your usual route, this incident affects how confident you are to find your way home. One of many important lessons from adjusting to sight loss, is to ask for help, then it is possible to forget the long, lonely struggle.

Take the next step

Carry your rainbow colours of hope, painted into a magnificent aura that surrounds your situations with purpose. Think about those colours while you decide on a new angel number. The subject of the next sensory journey, is relevant to your feelings of self-worth.

Angel 16 of New Opportunities

The angel of new-opportunities is number sixteen, she has a comforting smile, and a warm glow around her golden hair. She opens up a wooden box that contains the vision of a path in front of you. She asks you gently to take in the feeling of space and light quietly, as you sit for a while to observe people passing you by.

Angel number sixteen helps you to piece together the jigsaw puzzle of your life. She shows you each magical piece, one at a time. When you are ready, you can look into these moving images and connect them with others to explore the different outcomes.

You will discover that each scenario has a new story. She asks you to see the bigger picture and clears the way for you to see that some challenging experiences, actually have a reason for being there. She asks you to look closely at those rebellious pieces because they also have their place. It may not be what you had wanted at the time, but they actually lead you to better things in your life. Without these challenges, you would not be where you are, or who you are now. You need to feel the sense of achievement that comes with winning. Some pieces fit naturally to complement each other and like all good jigsaws, it may take years of time and patience to complete, until the final picture fills your heart with satisfaction, because it makes perfect sense to you.

Rainbow skies

Soak up the holiday atmosphere of the Bournemouth Gardens in Dorset. As you inhale the mouth-watering aroma of sweet sugared hot doughnuts, that wafts temptingly through the air, as you join the humming crowd of youths that display gaudy hair colours and sophisticated perfumed ladies, that walk beside careful elderly couples who are happy to take their time.

All the colourful people trail through the busy park that bursts with the glorious form of giant palm trees that stand in the middle of manicured flower displays. These flamboyant flowers appear to dance exotically in circles. Strong red and burnt orange helenium's parade side by side with the tall spiked foliage of dragon trees and pale-yellow dahlias that tower proudly over gold and copper marigolds, delicately lacing this dramatic lawn. Marching lines of pansies edge the walk way, rooted deeply in freshly dug soil that tempts a small child to plant a footprint or two. She is fascinated by her prints, as she gazes at the flowers that define this path that leads, all the way down to Bournemouth-seafront.

Imagine that you can hear the people passing by, in a rush of motion. Buzzing excitement is carried along with the lingering smell of hot doughnuts. This holiday aroma blends with the upbeat hum of chatter, interrupted by the occasional outbreak of laughter. The disruptive shout of a rowdy teenage boy with a throaty, newly broken voice chases his brother, who is escaping on a brightly painted skate board. Dodging through the people in an irregular manner and startling the oncoming crowd.

Settling down into a rhythm again, the hum of the crowd Is calm. Spaces become more obvious while you notice a tall, casually dressed young man, who carries a relaxed demeanour. Leaning slightly down to listen to his partner, who he protects closely with a gentle arm around her waist. She talks and gestures with her right hand as she describes her thoughts in great detail, her words disappearing into the atmosphere. She holds an ambitious tension through her shoulders that seems to float away with the breeze that ruffles her blue dress. Still more tension is lifted with the movement of her loose, medium length red hair as she looks up to demonstrate her dreams. He listens intently, sometimes replying with short answers which puzzle her.

Fortunately, he is completely wrapped up in her words, animated by the song of her accent, he lovingly lingers on every tone and takes time to work out what she means to say, he continues to protect her closely with a gentle arm around her waist. They walk arm in arm, carried on a breeze while they watch the changing sky that depicts cascading rainbows, that cross together through a blue sky. With trails of watermark footsteps like those of a child, circling the red sun. Multiple rainbows appear, one inside the other, caused by light waves. The couple are transformed by this symbolic sky that brings their dreams to life and gives them hope for their future together.

The chariot of progression

The chariot, in the major arcana of the tarot, asks you to use your calm attitude in romantic interactions, to create a happy compromise. Balance is called for now, to stabilise your most important relationship.

You don't need to settle for second best, a situation that can be easily resolved is always worth the effort, do so before it becomes more complicated. Ask your partner to give you the closeness and emotional attention that you both crave. Support for each other doesn't always happen easily, sometimes a gentle reminder is all that is needed.

Connect with other people by internet and phone, instead of long travel by car, rail or plane. If you do need to travel, check all fine details and structure your plans to cover all possibilities, taking care of your loved ones always.

Take the next step

The rainbow is an extremely positive sign, understood by young and old alike, a symbol of transformation and filled with hope for golden opportunities. Ask to be guided in the right direction while you select an angel number for your next sensory journey.

Angel 17 of Reflection

The angel of reflection is number seventeen, he draws close to show you infinite vitality and a free spirited, youthful attitude that enables your ideas to flow, so they can be expressed in a fresh and enthusiastic way.

Look for inspiration to balance all of your qualities, so that they work together to complement each other successfully. Make an effort to be understood by others and pay special attention to criticism because these testing times are your learning and the complements are your trophies for continuing inspiration.

Look back to the future

Explore the North Dorset trailway at Blandford in Dorset. Use this as an example of how far you have progressed. Your star qualities are reflected on the path in front of you today. Look back at the ground that you have trodden so many times, that your feet have left their impression. Play back your life as it has changed over many years and still, you are drawn here to reflect.

If only the trees could whisper your story, as they watch overhead, forming the same shaped arches, replicated from the railway tunnels that stand dark and far too silently while eerily vacant of trains. A memory can be as strong as reality because your Imagination enlarges everything, brings to life the smallest event and can be made as loud and dramatic, as a steam trains rhythm.

You imagine that the old steam train clatters into Blandford station, where it grinds to a slow stop with squealing breaks and sprays a fog of hissing steam across the platform. The air is charged with anticipation, as groups of teenage boys, dressed in smart black blazers and matching trousers, white shirts and neatly knotted ties, make their journey to school. Parents with their young children stand back to admire the train as it approaches in magnificent form, immaculately painted in bottle green. You imagine that the carriages wait patiently for you to pull open the handle.

The door opens towards you smoothly and it is a pleasant surprise to find two metal steps, that lead you up into the welcoming carriage that has a faint aroma of tobacco. The window seat is waiting for you to relax back, into the supportive sprung seat, that on closer inspection is covered in traditional moquette fabric, in orange and brown stripes. You admire the brown painted window frames and the pale cream curved carriage ceiling. Each seat has a table, ideal for map reading or hurried homework.

You imagine the gangs of school boys with strong attitudes, quiffed hair and shiny shoes, crowding into the carriage on the first day of term.

The door opens to let each eager boy in. Crashing closed repeatedly, until the station master announces over the tannoy speakers that, "this train is for Shillingstone and Sturminster Newton." This is not a quiet journey, although the sound is more bearable when the chatter of boys, merges into a comfortable chorus. Although your attention is focused on Lee, who is known for being the class bully and loves rivalry. He plays rummy with a younger boy called Jack, who has short fair hair and wears a tidy blazer and shorts.

Jack wins the game and hearing a cold silence, looks up slowly at Lee. He watches the older boys face change from calm contemplation, to become invaded by angry creases that furrow his brow while his expression becomes cold and freezes in a tight-lipped grimace. Lee is a sore loser and swipes the pack on the floor in a temper, keeping one card firmly under his shoe. Jack, who is blinking back tears, rubs his eyes and reaches towards Lee's shoe.

When everyone turns to stare with a deafening silence, Lee lifts his foot, releasing the card. He Kicks Jacks glass lined thermos-flask down the carriage, as the train whistles twice while chugging along through the rolling fields. Idyllic scenery that is ignored by Lee, who is a tall lad with a drooping fringe. He chews gum tediously and smirks to himself, as the cards with animal pictures on the back, are scattered under the table.

Jack is still on his hands and knees, trying to retrieve each one while the train rocks and shudders as it slows to a halt at Shillingstone station. Jack's eyes become wider, as he admires the platform heels and elegant legs of a lady who enters the carriage. He cowers under the sprung seats, where he feels repulsed by the circles of stuck on chewing gum. Jack wishes he could stay in hiding, although he catches the soft eyes of the lady, who has the kindest face he has ever seen. Bravely, he stands up, brushes down his shorts and feeling the ladies gaze, he turns around to pick up the smashed flask that is lying against the carriage door. He keeps his tearful eyes fixed to the floor and breathes in sharply when his eyes focus on large, black shoes, that are worn by a man. Then his eyes move up to see smart trousered legs and the comfortably belted waist of a conductor. Jack looks up bravely into his face and feels relieved to see that he has smiling eyes. This gentleman lays a large, friendly hand on Jack's shoulder and releases the calm, reassuring words. "We're nearly there," go and get your bag."

The floppy haired youth kick's the young boy's satchel at him from under the table then hands it to Jack silently with a look of sullen remorse.

The school day has only just begun for this young boy, who quickly opens the door to leave at Sturminster Newton station, watched by the bully who knows no other way to behave. He admires the sensitivity of children that are loved and wishes he had a quiet home to return to, without chaos and unpredictable explosions of temper from his parents. Lee doesn't know what to do with himself and will do anything for attention, because he gets noticed that way. He knows that he is important, so he must be recognised as being powerful and in charge. His smart shoes and new satchel give the impression that he has everything he needs and shows everyone else that he is alright. Maybe it is now, as he hangs his head low and focuses on the platform in front of him. His head hurts because he can't concentrate, but he will just keep on trying at school and when he leaves, he plans to get a job at the Post Office so that he can leave home one day.

As you leave this daydream, to return to the present day, you read on the sign outside Shillingstone station, that it closed in 1966 and has been sympathetically restored to a "living museum" by volunteers.

Sturminster Newton station also closed in 1966, now the site for business premises. Blandford railway station, that was once a fixture in the community, a source of employment and transport for all, was demolished in 1978 with only a few graffiti covered arches and a small section of monumental track remaining. It has been taken over by nature and functions as Blandford Forum trailway, a peaceful nature reserve where a wide path has replaced railway sleepers, between the steep chalk banks that once housed station platforms. An old, familiar walk that is always fresh and beautiful. Look back with understanding, as people from the past join your thoughts to remind you to look forwards with wisdom and see your qualities with a smile. Everything evolves, just as this path was once a busy station and now a haven for wildlife and a place for the community to enjoy its serene tranquillity.

Strength of character

Reflection is represented by strength in the major arcana of the tarot. Always take charge of your fears and desires so that they work for you and no longer hinder your progress. Your vulnerability is your greatest strength. Learn from it, as you rest and recover. You continue to grow as you become stronger with each day that you believe in yourself.

Ideas happen when you rest. This is valuable time for making plans. Sometimes your creations happen, or they may not come to anything at all. That depends on your health and circumstances, but never dismiss an idea completely, because you just, never know what is around the corner.

~ 72 ~

Take the next step

Imagine that you are resting in a comfortable hammock that hangs between the trees. Slowly it swings from left to right, until a new angel number appears in your mind, showing you the way to your next sensory journey.

Angel 18 of the Universe

The angel of the universe is number eighteen, this universal life force holds out a hand to you that is associated with childhood. He takes you back to feeling your way, like a baby who needs support, everything is new and challenging. Your first step out into the universe is full of exciting possibilities, it is one where you discover the rhythm of life in your own time.

The magic hat

Make positive dreams come alive while you visit the abandoned Tyneham village, on the Lulworth Cove. Investigate the old school rooms that still echo with children's voices left behind, when the whole village community was evacuated to safety, as World War two began.

During their nature lesson, all the children were instructed calmly by their teacher, to leave their work books and desks, to put down their pen s and paper, then line up quietly by the front door.

They left behind their wooden desks with full ink wells, abandoned pens and pencils still wait for their return. A silent cloak room with empty name pegs is eerily still, holding onto the fear that the children felt, when they grabbed their coats, then ran outside with marbles rolling around in their pockets, as the stern teacher sent them straight home to be with their families.

The people of Tyneham had to leave their beloved homes and village behind, as the families and their pets were evacuated, in a dreadful hurry. In usual times the children would go down to the beach on a warm, afternoon like this. It is the most beautiful beach you have ever seen, with white rocks and transparent blue waters, that gleam invitingly. It is ideal for swimming and the beach has many hidden fossils to discover. The children spent many hours here, playing hide and seek as they chased back through the trees, with wet shorts and vests clinging to their agile bodies. The chorus of sheep and cows in the background was comforting for the children, who's families worked on the farm land there. Just before they reached home, they would often stop to visit the theatre, which was always open for them to practice their drama performances.

If you could imagine you were one of them, would you join in? Would you take part in the production with the children? Maybe you would be the star of the show, the one never to be forgotten. If you choose, here is a stage for you to perform. Here is a place where childhood dreams are kept forever. Caught up in your childhood magic, imagine that your dreams are the biggest and brightest of all.

You imagine that you are living your dreams as you act them out. Spell-bound by their power, you pause for a deep breath and reflect on how much you can magnify these images. You stand with poise on the stage, elegantly wearing a black top hat while holding a special magic wand in your right hand.

You paint with the wand, spontaneously forming the picture of your beautiful visions and as you do so, you feel wonderful. You are in control of everything that happens from this moment onwards. You use the wand to direct all of your amazing visions into the hat and then you wave your hand over the top to seal them in place. The hat is golden and bright, as you hold it respectfully, because you know that all of the universe has given you these dreams and you are grateful for all that you have now and in the coming years. You know that you have all of the tools that you need, to be true to yourself from now on.

The World of opportunities

The world is symbolised in the major arcana of the tarot, as being a place full of opportunities, although your most comfortable place can be just as fulfilling because you have the whole world of dreams at your fingertips.

A bed time meditation to help you to sleep peacefully, while you allow yourself to remember your dreams. As you drift towards sleep, you may wish to let your creativity flow with a bright vision of moving coloured waves. Mesmerising, moving white, blue and pink light floods your imagination, as you relax while you feel angels close by, in the depths of the stillness. You can look up, lean forwards and spread out your arms widely with the force of intention.

Your dream may become more vivid still, as you are swept high up, to ride the back of the mystical creature, Pegasus the winged horse. His back is more comfortable than the warmest of beds and you relax more while sinking into the softest, most luxurious, of all dreamy colours that envelop you like blankets that are reminiscent of a swirling river. You hold on tightly as you fall down to rest on a cloud in the blue sky.

As you lie back on the soft, floating cloud of colours. A yellow haze glows warmly around your back, soothing every ache away.

You don't have to hold your eyes open because Pegasus is in your dreams as a stallion and with your eyes wide open, you can dream and if you are relaxed enough to dream with your eyes open, you will see that he is still as white as the stars.

He bows right down to you, his hot, steaming breath blows fiercely on your icy, cold face, you desperately want to remember this dream, even though you are tired and you just want to drift. Don't forget to remember him, as he stretches out an expanse of soft, silky feathered wings, you realise that he listens to your thoughts.

He takes your breath away as you watch him fly up into the expanding night sky, climbing higher still, while sweeping a three-dimensional trail of light. He paints diamond pictures that gleam and shine brightly.

With a stretch of his wings, he illuminates a star dust formation in the image of a mother. She is holding her precious new born baby close to her chest. Below her, the small world is highlighted with light that delicately frames the maternal universe that is your home, like your mother's womb, where you are floating peacefully, in a place where you can choose to remember your dreams, although you don't have to sleep until you are ready to let go.

~ 77 ~

Take the next step

Discover that your chosen path is your best friend. There is
nothing to be afraid of. Have courage and go for it today.
Reflect on the universe as you choose a new angel number to
take you on your next sensory journey.

Angel 19 of Empathy

The angel of empathy is number nineteen, he puts his arms around you and asks you to be empathic with someone in need, who appears to be very different from yourself. You may be surprised to find that the person that you are supporting, has a very good rapport with you which is the foundations for remarkable progress. Angel number nineteen asks you to be empathic with others that are not like yourself.

The flight of a Buzzard

Explore the home of the buzzard, at Wareham Forest in Dorset where you will discover how it might feel to be a buzzard in flight, a kingfisher hovering over the water and a minnow, swimming in a bubbling stream. When you have finished your journey, you will feel comfortable and relaxed in your own body.

Imagine that you are a buzzard, escaping from the ground to soar over the white mist where the earth seems to be a distant dream. The moist clouds resemble endless mountain peaks that carry you higher. You swoop through an opening in the feather duster sky, to survey agricultural fields, stretching out in front of you. As you travel, you watch scattered sheep grazing the expanse of lush, grass meadows, that boast dense hedgerows, in all shades of green and burnt sienna earth tones. Deep charcoal shadows define the rows of crops, in richly fertile soil. You see a flash of movement and rapidly descend on a small rabbit, your eyes glinting with disappointment as it vanishes into a warren of underground tunnels.

You listen to the trickling motion of a meandering stream that flows beside the field. As a bird of prey, you are fixated by moving shapes defined by shadows, opening up in moving sunlight, to display rich colours.

As a plant, you twine around bushes for good company and settle your twining roots down into the earth, to drink deeply from the river bed.

As a Kingfisher you hover in blue, orange and a hint of green, all in a blur of fast-moving colours, hovering still, while fanning geometric patterns with the whirring speed of your flashing wings.

Water burbles, sparkles and bubbles. Carrying you now, as you are one in a shoal of minnows that slide around pebbles in a continuous flourish of movement. You are drifting from left to right as part of the clear, life-giving water. Surging left to right gliding through the twisted branches of a scrambling, wild rose bridge.

Become aware of your beautiful toes and your hips, how fluid they are as you return to your human form. Your body knows now that your life force is energy. You flow, move, grow and breathe. Feel nurtured by the earth while you breathe in then breathe out and rest while you listen to the robin as he sings his familiar song.

Take the next step

We are all different and can never be the same, although our differences may lead to conflict, we can still find a solution if we are willing to try. Even if there is only a small amount of support to be given, we can do so in a caring and understanding way. Think about what the word empathy means to you while you choose a new angel number, then turn to the next sensory journey, to discover what areas of your life need some empathy today.

Angel 20 of Joy

The angel of joy is number twenty, she prompts you to balance your body and mind, by taking a physical exercise challenge today. This may be to go for a swim at the nearest heated pool, set yourself a target to see how many lengths you can swim.

A different challenge could be a fast walk to a favourite landmark, that is at least a mile away. Time yourself on your stop watch, all the way there and back again. Whatever you choose to do, make it fun and this may be the start of a new exercise routine to keep your body and mind in balance.

A blindfolded walk

A sensory view of the historical market town of Salisbury in Wiltshire. You are so excited to experience this challenge, that has been set by the Royal National Institute of Blind People and the Guide dogs' charity, which is to wear a tight, black blindfold, just for an hour. Regular blindfold events are held to highlight the dangers of street obstructions, to those with sight discover, makes you tremble
with anticipation and your nerves are   as your sighted guide Elizabeth sweeps her long, auburn hair away from her face and secures the black cloth tightly around your head. When she places her smooth palm on your forehead, she feels beads of warm sweat that dampen her fingers. She smiles with her

calming voice, as she asks you to trust her completely and then everything will be alright.

The loud boom of traffic echoes from the rows of medieval houses and inns, that stand alongside modern, flat fronted shops. With many busy roads to negotiate, you feel clumsy and vulnerable while holding Elizabeth's arm because she is not used to guiding you. Even though you can feel the warmth of her body next to yours, your heightened sensitivity gives you a sudden chill, as you walk through the shelter of the fourteenth century Poultry Cross monument, you touch one of the pillars and the shudder caused by the cold stone, connects you with a time long past. When you walk left into Minster Street, you feel the presence of medieval times, as the ancient lives blend with the modern society of today.

Then you approach the market square, where you notice that the temperature warms, as you feel the welcoming sunlight on your face and step back to make way for bustling crowds of people that energise the atmosphere completely. Echoing footsteps clatter and scuff along aged flag stones that line the narrow passageway that leads to a vast traditional market square.

Touching your hand gently, Elizabeth traces your fingers through hers, fanning them out on the bark of a large tree. She fastens the belt of her long, suede coat while she explains that during the winter months, Christmas decorations of sparkling, coloured lights climb the sturdy trunk. As she speaks, you can imagine the sparkle in her eyes, as they light up while she thinks about the bright Christmas lights. As you stand by the tree, your lack of vision brings you closer to her, as you are more aware of how she stands, the lack of tension in her body and the sound of her breathing that is soft and reassuring.

You turn to listen to the men who cry out to sell their wares, by making friendly music with their warm Wiltshire farmer tones. "Come and get your apples and bunches of bananas. Fresh oranges, six for a pound." The sound grabs your attention as they shout out for all to hear again. Then they blend into the background, as you listen to the clinking of cutlery and clattering of shiny, white plates being stacked up high. You are completely drawn into the joyful sounds of happily busy people and the sing-song voices of children, who are walking beside their parents while talking non-stop to get their undivided attention. This effortless chorus of life is so fascinating that your balance is distracted and you knock your hip against a table that rattles and shakes as the contents slide, narrowly missing the floor.

Elizabeth tugs on your elbow, to pull you away although you stop still. The silence is waiting for your apology. You fill the awkward gap quickly with a firm "I'm sorry," then receive a mumbled reply of "that's okay," spoken with a gruff throaty voice that gives you the impression of an elderly gentleman with plenty of zest for life. You hear the clinking chain of a lead being dragged along the grey cobble stones, as a small dog anticipates a treat from his generous owner.

Chair legs scrape and plastic bags rustle while you hear the warm tones of Wiltshire and Dorset accents mingling together, as the local lady's que up to ask the country butcher for duck eggs, bacon and ham. The smoky barbeque aroma of hot dogs and onions wafts through the air while the frying pan crackles and sizzles temptingly close by.

The noisy hum of people increases here, making you feel extremely tired. Where is Elizabeth? She has turned her back and in your panic at being alone, you call out for her. In her excitement at finding herbs at a plant stall, she has been distracted. She places her hand in yours to apologise, she rubs sage and rosemary between your fingers. Fragrant basil and tactile tomato plants are quite overwhelming at this moment.

You suddenly feel helpless, weak and exhausted. Elizabeth asks you to take a deep breath in, count to ten and breathe out. "I am alright," you whisper to her breathlessly while you walk on and stop again, fighting the fact that the world seems to be spinning out of control.

You have tolerated the dark blindfold for long enough, so you ask Elizabeth to untie it for you. With huge relief as it falls away from your face, you see that everything is just as your imagination had shown, although you are glad to shake off the feeling of fatigue and dizziness. You are filled with a rush of joy, to have experienced this unique perspective on life and hug Elizabeth tightly while you thank her with the warmth of your heart.

The force of the sun

The sun is an important symbol of joy in the major arcana of the tarot. Imagine that you are walking out of Salisbury, along the water meadows. With views of the cathedral and its beautiful spire, that points straight up to the blue sky and slowly fades into the cold distance. You reach the warm sunshine, with the sound of the market place humming in your ears. As you walk further into the sun, the high-pitched note of traffic fades away. Now you can hear the blackbirds and you are surrounded by the honey pine green, of trees that appear in abstract form. The city is a memory now, a distant murmur.

The sunshine here is warming and tells a story of times past by. Dark lines represent the structure of woodland, blasting through the stillness of this vast field. As the sun's rays mix with a damp haze, the light play reveals the brightness and form of an angel. The dazzling red and yellow form, cancels the shadows that are cast. Elevated with scorching red wings, the body a swirl of blue and yellow, as the birds and the wind are silent to listen. Just as suddenly, the light changes and the angel merges into different forms of light, scattered in all directions, then the birds begin to sing again, as you radiantly absorb the joy of this moment.

Take the next step

Keep a sense of joyful accomplishment, as you take the sun to shine over your projects and bring positive energy into your next sensory journey, as you choose a new angel number.

Angel 21 of Vulnerability

The angel of vulnerability is number twenty-one, his refreshing influence gently reminds you that courage starts with showing up and letting yourself be noticed. However scary that may be, if you have the courage to be vulnerable, you are open to everything therefore must believe in yourself. Consequently, your attitude to life, love, parenting and leadership can be transformed for the better.

Angel number twenty-one in relation to vulnerability, carries a message to let go of your usual routine for a few days. Bring all of your abilities into focus so that you can think about them all. Polish and practice your favourite ability until your expression flows and your authority sparkles persistently with a touch of magic in your hands.

The Beach House

A weekend break at the Beach House Hotel at Milford on Sea in Hampshire. As you approach your destination, your partner drives patiently while waiting for a quiet moment to recover after a long journey, full of conversation and silly jokes, that can only be funny once. The car turns a corner slowly and the crunch of gravel signals your arrival on an open drive. He easily finds a parking space where you both wait in silence, as a burst of heavy rain fall interrupts, to perform a magnificent display of diamond light droplets, that fall with a deafening force that could be compared to millions of pebbles, crashing down to earth.

You listen as the orchestra of rain slows in rhythm then pauses to let the howling, gale force winds take charge of the chorus, as they sweep giant sea waves up to reach frothy, high peaks that drop suddenly, to crash menacingly and with magnificent force against grey concrete barriers. The atmosphere is fresh and invigorating, even while you both sit in the stuffy car interior and you wait, until your partner looks at you with large, gentle eyes and gestures to the door while asking if you are ready to leave.

Lancelot's house is your holiday home for a few days, named after the big, friendly ginger cat that lives there. The welcome mat looks like it may be a day time bed for this friendly character to take a nap, before he strolls across to visit the hotel guests for breakfast, lunch and tea.

You are completely unfamiliar with this new place and feel incredibly vulnerable, although these feelings disappear when the white front door opens to reveal a soft, yellow light that shines on a newly carpeted staircase that leads up to a welcoming entrance hall. You are grateful to find that it smells like fresh linen and you begin to relax when you see two warm and inviting bedrooms, freshly cleaned with a faint aroma of bath soap that lingers pleasantly. They are decorated with distressed pine furniture, calmly you run your hands over the smooth wood, to feel the worn quality and you enjoy the fact that everything is stunningly showcased with subtle lighting. A seaside theme is in keeping with the beach location, as a collection of starfish ornaments, drift wood and pottery lighthouses are thoughtfully presented throughout. You find the reference to sailing interesting, with stand-alone features of twisted rope lamp stands and white wood panels, that remind you of a boat. You relax still more to the background rhythm of churning waves, that can be heard through large, picture framed windows. Then you notice how the tidy beds feel clean and warm, as you sink down into the softest feather pillows and appreciate the plump, duvet that moulds around your back. You touch the crisp, clean white linen that hugs your legs and supports your arms so that they feel like they are floating on soft, white clouds of warm comfort. You close your eyes while the radio plays soothing classical music, you allow yourself to rest completely while you sink deeply, into this blissfully comfortable bed. Sleep refreshes and heals every ache in your body, a deeply satisfying slumber that seems to linger and soothe your body endlessly, keeping your muscles loosely relaxed and heavy.

When you awaken from this dreamy bliss, you are bright and happy to see that dusk has brought peace from the driving rain. You hear your partners soft breathing while he is lying beside you, his hand in yours and when he wakes, you both listen to the crashing sea waves from the safety of this comfortable bed.

In the darkening sky, the Victorian hotel is large and imposing, illuminated by flood lights that reveal natural lawns, that frame a gravel drive. Elegant steps lead up to a welcoming, enclosed porch that offers security from the elements. A footpath runs beside the hotel and tall grass grows on the sand, that dips and rises unexpectedly. You walk together carefully, until your senses take over in the darkness of this place. Your balance stabilises while you both feel the way, holding each other tightly while the crashing and surging rhythm of sea waves, excite you while gale force winds sweep up sand clouds, that make you feel vulnerable and free.

He reaches out to hold your arm, as you sway on the uneven sand dunes that cave in under foot. In these turbulent conditions that are charged with a wild, healing vitality. You feel no urge to be anywhere else while the satisfaction of salt tasting spray, showers your face and your hair is blown ragged in all directions. You don't need to rush, even though your eyes sting and your nose is wet and cold to the touch. In these challenging conditions he holds onto you tightly and squeezes your fingers reassuringly. You can feel the force of mother nature before you. Her rhythm and motion, holds a terrifying power that silences you to listen, so that you can be truly aware of your vulnerability while you are in her hands. Your partner is beside you, his hand in yours while you listen to the crashing sea waves from this comfortable place and you appreciate his arms that mould themselves around your body while your legs are supported against his and feel like they are floating on soft, white clouds of warm comfort and you close your eyes to savour, a precious moment of renewal.

The High Priestess

The high priestess in the major arcana of the tarot is a young woman, with a pale complexion and short, wavy brown hair that reveals her pale arms, perfectly hugging her familiar shapely lean, as the breeze smooths the folds of her moss green dress. One porcelain hand is held over her heart while the other delicately rests behind her ear to listen. She burrows her bare toes into the sandy earth, to soak up the precious warmth while her eyes remain closed and her peaceful lips wear her feminine expression. Her short, wavy hair is ruffled by the breeze, as the tall shadows come out to play. When the sun light retreats, she remains balanced and serene.

The high priestess is an important guide of everlasting change. An ice Queen, with a heart of gold. She has the ability to reason with destiny, as she works with love while a fiery furnace echoes her fire and ice soul. She knows that their opposing nature threatens to extinguish each of them, although they always survive separately in respect of each other. On the surface she is peaceful and serene with a mystical quietness. This spiritual teacher is strong and wise. Her balanced approach stems from her vulnerability, which enables change to sit comfortably in her arms.

Take the next step

Stay here to breathe in a moment of renewal before leaving, so that you can feel the whole of mother nature before you. An exciting amount of permissive exposure with an open heart is healing, in rhythm and motion. The message of vulnerability continues into your next sensory journey, as you choose a new angel number.

Angel 22 of Expression

The angel of expression is number twenty-two, she is as steady and firm as the ground under your feet, stability is her reassuring message. Keep to what you know and wait for your finances to improve, before making any major changes. Stay steady and stable on the path of security. When the time is right, you can be brave with your ambitions, for now keep them fresh and vibrant in your dreams.

The power of touch

The power of touch is so positive, many massage therapists swear by it as an alternative medicine. When someone else holds you, in a nurturing way, and takes the weight off your body for just a little while, it is like giving yourself permission to recover. Trusting a massage therapist to look after you, is like allowing them to work with you, to let you rest, so you can gain your strength again.

There is a way to write about massage, but it proved to be quite difficult. It is a very intimate subject, yet practical and essential. In effect, the massage therapist nurtures your body, mind and spirit. Here are my words about a massage.

Your eyes speak while wide awake and amplify the volume of your gaze, until they relax. Your warm hands are tired, as they are so busy. Their lived in quality holds attention, moulded by your work, telling an intriguing and captivating story. You use them to gesture expressively while you speak. Fan out your words and smooth them over, to add reassuring validation. Drawing spoken words in the air clarifies the meaning of speech, that is otherwise suggestive and open to interpretation.

Facial expression is like a book to be read and explored with touch. Every contour of the face, smooths out when relaxed. Then with the slightest tension, tightens and creases. The jaw is tight with unspoken words while the furrowed brow has a line for each question. The worries fade away, with rain drop touches from gentle fingertips and the lines on the forehead are softened still more, by the firm pressure of the palms, silky to the touch of firm hands that sweep down to smooth the magnificent jaw line. Chiselled with sculptural squareness, defining a smile or a frown.

You are a work of art with a balanced, dramatic posture. Your movements perform an individual dance, a strong shapely silhouette that can never be ignored. Instead, dramatized with the expression of a physical language, that is a beautiful interpretation of your own being.

The Magicians wand

The magician, in the major arcana of the tarot appears in an abstract, fluid form and vibrant moving colours. He commands a deeply masculine influence to be greatly respected. Look at him as a motivational figure, who uses new ideas to overcome challenges. He is not one to follow the crowd, instead he has developed his own bag of tricks to see him through. Prepared for all eventualities, he has gained in wisdom through trial and error. He teaches that your voice must be heard and your views spoken with passion while directed with your positive energy, as if with a powerful, magical wand to guide your unique perspectives.

Take the next step

Under the influence of the magician, the gift of magic is in your hands. Relax and release any doubts about your progress, as you choose a new angel number for your next sensory journey.

Angel 23 of Honesty

The angel of honesty is number twenty-three. He opens a book of new learning today. If you are drawn to a particular subject, now is a good time to develop your skills further, make notes of your progress along the way because learning should never be wasted. Think about your home and look at your daily routines more closely, to improve your household energy bills. Think about what you dispose of in the waste bin, some creative upcycling can benefit your finances, health and that of the world you live in.

Stepping stones

The peaceful Compton acres gardens at Poole in Dorset, are well worth a visit. An attractive wooden bridge leads to a water garden, where you can climb the many stone steps that lead into shaded fern glades, that are overshadowed by mature trees that reach out their branches, to provide a roof like canopy while the rainbow colours, shine through the misty spray of cascading water, that is captured in the sunshine. The wild movement of the living water, chases between each flat, shiny rock while

you balance on the first stone and watch your wobbling legs falter in apprehension. The gurgling sounds of the flourishing spring seem to laugh at them. You realise that the slippery stones are the only way across the vast pond. Alive with Chinese water lilies and swirling with giant Angel Koi that seek attention while they splash on the surface with wide-open mouths. There is a certain amount of risk if you place your foot wrongly, so you question whether you should continue, or turn back to dry land.

You realise that if you slip when your foot touches down on the smooth, wet stones, you will fall into the water then you will pick yourself up, dry yourself off and laugh about it later. If you return to the bridge, you have been defeated by fear which has no reason to win this time. You watch the Angel Koi with wide-open mouths and make your decision carefully.

The Queen of laughter

The Queen of laughter will help you to see life from an honest perspective. You may have noticed that people with a natural sense of humour have a busy life. Everyone wants to be around them as much as possible because laughter, is the best way to be open with each other. Some of the benefits of laughter are: the wonderful relief of tension that encourages honesty that is expressed with physical warmth. Laughter can improve your health, as it triggers positive emotional and physical changes in the body that relieve pain. A good laugh encourages your body to recover more quickly from illness. In fact, the act of genuine laughter rocks the whole energy system of the human aura and begins to shift heavy, negative stagnant energy then starts to refresh the energetic layers of the auric layer, with new vibrational strength.

Take the next step

Honesty is when you see yourself for who you really are, the water always reflects what you are scared to show. As the stepping stones to your next path are stretching out in front of you now. Imagine that the angel number for your next sensory journey is written on the first stone that you step on. When you are ready, take the next step forwards.

Angel 24 of Mothers

The angel of mothers is number twenty-four, she is a serene symbol of someone with a caring nature. Positively giving every day, reflecting how good It is for her psychology, to be rewarded with payment and gratitude for her efforts.

She reminds you that you must be well and happy to continue your quality of life. Let go of suffering for your family and share the work load together with laughter. When you support your family strongly, you will be taken seriously and with the beauty of respect.

A Mother's view

Situated in the valleys surrounding Blandford Forum and hidden under the cover of scattered woodland, Hod hill is just waiting to be explored. You may have thought of visiting, or you can continue on this journey, that involves the company of a baby. Although it could still be just an idea, a little seed of thought. Discovering your maternal side may surprise you and with this on your mind, imagine just for today that you have your own precious baby to care for.

Now that there are two of you, everything has to be achieved together which may be a challenging concept. A very comfortable, well fitted sling supports your baby up high on your back. The belt is tight around your waist and shoulder straps are adjusted so that he does not slip.

Your dog runs ahead, she pauses to look back at you, taking on the responsibility of both of you. As you catch up with her, you appreciate your walking boots that tread the woodland floor, that is deeply coated in autumn leaves. They are dappled in the golden splendour of sunlight, that delicately touches the edges of tree trunks and highlights the black, cracked bark and the movement of your dog's fur, as she touches her wet nose against your hand.

Extreme rain fall has caused flooding in places and an incredible amount of mud, seems to be sliding down the hill towards you. As you step forwards, the steep slope is unforgiving. Your knees are wet with dense, stickiness so you put your hands down to the ground to balance your weight and that of your baby.

You smile at your dog who was once white and is now almost totally black, from the paws upwards. You touch your baby's small bowed legs that are warm and hang loosely while he sleeps soundly. His hands are delicate and open wide enough for you to place your forefinger in his palm. He instinctively curls his fingers around yours. You reach behind to feel his head, which is lolling over to the left and he seems to become heavier while he sleeps. You shuffle your back to distribute his weight more evenly, feeling the relentless pull on your shoulders.

Scrambling up ahead, your dog's ears flap as she runs, her tail held high with pure delight and her tongue pants a breathless "come on."

A surprising shift in the climate takes hold, as you reach the highest point, causing a damp fog to wrap around your shoulders. Grey shapes hover and lurk, as the fog shrouds everything. The chilled breeze is cooling and calming, although your nose and cheeks tingle, as you push further into this cloud, that seems to mix with wide, white beams of sunlight.

The sun evaporates the grey shadows and illuminates an expanse of grassland. A rich habitat for wild flowers, birds, butterflies and moths. Bright and beautiful, alive with colour and vibrant richness. Your baby snuffles and whines then kicks his small foot that causes his shoe to fall to the ground. As you bend down to feel where it might be, your dog nudges something in the grass and retrieves the shoe. You stroke the clever dog fondly, shaping her soft head with your hands to tell her that she is amazing.

Your baby is safe and secure on your back, you can feel each movement of his breathing, he is always with you, you are incredibly grateful for this special closeness.

The protective empress

The empress, in the major arcana of the tarot represents motherhood, she symbolizes the earth, an image that suggests a mother holds her child's hand for a short while, although she holds the love for that child in her heart forever. Don't forget that everyone needs that loving hand and indeed to be looked after, even if they are not easy to care for at all. Supported independence is the best way forwards for everyone.

You will be surprised at how many times there is someone looking out for you, every step of the way. Even if that someone, is a complete stranger. Maybe you ask for a hand over the road, or for directions to a new place. There is always someone standing right behind you when you really need them most of all.

Take the next step

Both men and women need to connect with their feminine energy. Mother earth encourages you to think of an angel number, that reminds you most of your favourite place on this earth. Use this as the number for your next sensory journey.

Angel 25 of Nurture

The angel of nurture is number twenty-five, he opens out the palms of his hands like butterfly wings, to show you that everything is there for you. Let your true colours develop and dry in the sun. Flaunt the presence of mind that you gain when you are in tune with your aura colours, as their beauty surrounds you.

Precious moments

Explore the beautiful Kingston Lacy gardens at Wimborne in Dorset. Imagine a precious moment to treasure while you tread, bare foot across the lush, green lawn that is soaked in diamond light dew.

As you walk through a forest of ancient trees, it feels like everything is growing around you. Sweet scented bluebells are mixed with the white flowers of wild garlic, that smells delicious when it brushes against your legs, as you walk through a forest of ancient trees.

The angels draw your attention to nurture what is important in so many ways. Now you are listening, hear them whispering in the breeze, "nurture your dreams, compare them to the sweet scent of the vibrant flowers that surround you." "Be quiet, you might awaken the new buds of tea roses, with delicate petals that tickle your fingertips and glint with baubles of morning dew."

You listen to a voice on the freshness of the breeze that comes and goes, it sounds like a woman's whisper. She seems to want you to understand that without nurture, the roses will shed their neglected petals and their shiny leaf points will dry and curl over in sadness. Just as your new dreams need to be fed and watered, until they burst into a colour wash of bright, floral enthusiasm. Treated with willing effort and celebrated when there is progress. Nurture all of the heavenly tulips that are nestled together, bathing in sunlight that blesses them lovingly with warmth. The play of light dusts over their damp petals, like precious, inspired dreams of children who sleep.

The guardian of children

The guardian of children reminds us that the concept of nurture is like a warm, endless hug that is invisible to the eye. A nurturing environment allows the child to know that they are always loved and protected. Young people who have a good start in life, are able to share their nurturing skills with others, providing a great support for those who really need a friend.

Parents and carers provide their children with food and water to nourish them, while they watch their young people grow and develop in their own ways. They allow them to have their own understanding of who they are. When young people are encouraged to express themselves, their confidence grows. When they are congratulated for their achievements, they know that they are lovable. This means that even when young people are struggling with problems, they still know that their family is there for them, and will not judge any mistakes they have made. After all they have to make their own way in life.

Take the next step

A gentle nudge or a huge mile-stone, both are reminders to look at the next stage in life. Hold on to thoughts about your future, nurture them, maybe they are possible. If not, find something that is achievable. There is a plan for you that is still to be discovered. Ask your angel to help you find it, as you choose a new angel number for your next sensory journey.

Angel 26 of Fathers

The angel of fathers is number twenty-six, he shows your intention to change your ideas into actual reality. The angel of fathers asks you to recognise your talents because you have so much to give. Travel and explore your fascinating surroundings, share your journeys with others while you learn from them, they can also learn from you.

The very distant rumble of dramatic thunder hangs in the heavy atmosphere, before the first warm, heavy drops of summer rainfall excites your strong need for adventure. Your drive to succeed is admirable because even if you lose your way, rest and recover then your ability to find a new direction will return.

With a survival kit packed, you scan the view across distant valleys. Breathe the air of the villages, sea and forests. Your new path is an intriguing challenge with spine tingling excitement as your motivation, nothing can stand in your way.

A message in a bottle

Enjoy the beach at Bridport in Dorset. Here you can take yourself right back in time and through the clearing clouds you can see a memory of yourself sitting on a quiet beach. With your legs outstretched and wide eyes squinting in the brightness, as you sit on a familiar, sandy blanket. You push down hard, into the soft sand with a blue plastic spade, while your father passes you warm sandwiches and a melting chocolate bar.

Then you watch in fascination, as he blows powerfully into an inflatable, rubber ring, until its red and white stripes expand into the shape of a large, plump doughnut. The orange and yellow striped wind break shelters you both from the gentle sea breeze.

You escape to run down to the water's edge, leaving footprints behind in the wet sand, you wonder why they disappear when you turn around to look. You chase the footprints round in circles and they still sink away completely.

At the water's edge, you gaze into the distance and detect a shiny object floating towards you. A clear, glass bottle drifts on the open water, floating in and out on the waves. The tide brings it closer to you and the sun glints brightly on the glass, illuminating its mystery.

Your father's hairy ankles are submerged in water, as he towers above you. The clear bottle with a faded label is within reach and just about visible through the glass, is a rolled-up piece of paper. Lying at your feet, the bottle bobs up and down, just asking to be retrieved. You quickly grab it, before it drifts away, feeling that this could be a great discovery. Maybe this could lead to a pirate's treasure trove, or even a secret message from a far-off land.

Your father helps you a little apprehensively, to unscrew the bottle cap. With the palm of your hand, you tap the base firmly, to knock out the tightly rolled cylinder of thin paper and untie the string that is wrapped around it. You unravel and read aloud the message.

"Message number twenty-six, if you have taken the time to read this note, you must also take time to convert your ideas into reality. The angels ask you to recognise your talents. You have so much to give, keep on looking for opportunities to learn about this world. Travel and explore, share your journeys then others will be inspired to explore in the future."

Your Father asks you to push the note inside the bottle for someone else to read. He takes the bottle from you and throws it out as far as he can while listening for the distant "splash" as it falls and watching as it skims the swelling wave patterns. Your father holds your hand warmly and reassuringly. His silence speaks louder than words, he doesn't need to say anything to you at all. At this moment, you know that one day you would like to be just like him.

You watch the tide swell and surge inland until evening falls, the changing tides represent your emotions, they ebb and flow with the cycles of the moon that rises over the horizon, as the sea air makes you feel more and more sleepy, you could just fall asleep here, to the sound of the waves churning endlessly.

The empowering emperor

The emperor in the major arcana of the tarot, represents a father's regimental discipline within his family. A protective instinct that stems from the moment that he held his new baby son for the very first time. He placed his golden hand on his delicate head and held the tiny baby gently and flopped him over his strong shoulder. A contented baby, full up after his first drink of life-giving milk. His mother wrapped him carefully in a soft, white shawl. Mesmerised by the love he felt for the mother of his son, he glowed with pride for both of them, a feeling that he kept close to his heart for ever more.

Take the next step

Keep your father in mind and understand him in a different light, as you think of a new angel number and collect your survival kit so that you can continue to explore your next sensory journey.

Angel 27 of Sexuality

The angel of sexuality is number twenty-seven. This masculine and feminine angel teaches that, as everything becomes more achievable with practice, you can easily gain respect and confidence in all areas of your life. In relation to sexuality, angel number twenty-seven draws attention to the fact that you do not leave your sexuality at home. Be aware of this and take it with you everywhere you go, so that you can feel proud of who you are.

An evening Swim

Submerge yourself in the waves at Sandbanks beach, Poole in Dorset. As you imagine that you are sitting beside the sea with your bare feet sinking into warm grains of sand. The cool, playful waves lap over your sensitive toes, tempting you to experience how the water feels when you swim with naked freedom. You release the security of your towel and allow the exhilarating chill to tempt every part of your body.

You powerfully swim out and let the turbulence balance you. Lifting you up and spontaneously throwing you back down again to taste the force of the sea. You close your eyes and give permission for the music of the water to wash through every delightful thought. The atmosphere feels sensual, as splashes of colour dart and play through the immersive depths of water. You ride the waves with each stroke pushing you weightlessly forwards, until your feet touch the shingle and seaweed of the shore. Released from the ocean waves. You wrap your heavy, shivering body in a warm towel that absorbs the salty water, dripping from your bare skin. You lie down on the sand, wrapped in the thick and comforting bath sheet. The warmth of yellow sunlight, penetrates through your glowing soul and soothes your elated consciousness.

Take the next step

You don't leave your sexuality at home; you take it with you. Not in a carrier bag, instead you wear it with pride. Your natural expression is indeed the essence of life itself. Keep sexuality on your mind and imagine your heart's desire. Then instinctively choose a new angel number and move forwards to your next sensory journey.

Angel 28 of Partners

The angel of partners is number twenty-eight, this angel raises you up on a platform, where all of your talents can be showcased. He encourages you to make a stage of your own. You can show your experience here and build on your learning by practising new ideas. Our self-critical minds need the balance and support that our human partners can give us with their positive encouragement. Look to your dogs, cats and other animals as complementary partners that are never judgemental and with plenty of play time, exercise and affection, the greater the rewards will be.

A guide dog's view

The remote village of Sturminster Marshall is our destination, as we ride on the X8 bus to Poole which is full of cheerful elderly people of all shapes and sizes. Squashed into bus seats, leaning in towards each other, listening intently and swapping conversation loudly, for those who are hard of hearing. They watch solemn students, heads who lean against shiny windows, wearing headphones and vacant gazes.

Mum flicks her long, dark hair out of her watery eyes. She is tired of the world, feeling exhausted and unloved. She has escaped to her favourite corner at the back, wearing her old daisy boots, jeans and a warm jacket, she cups her hands over her eyes to shield them from the sun.

I am a shiny, black Labrador-Retriever, who quietly lies at her feet. With a contented grumble, I put my head down on my soft, stretched-out paws and watch mum affectionately while I try to ignore the giggling child, who is eating cheese and onion flavoured crisps very loudly indeed. He drops one on the floor, so I position myself in a secret commando crawl and stretch my nose forwards just a little, to reach the crisp. He turns his head and his ears twitch with interest, as he notices me and reaches out a greasy hand to stroke my head while humming softly over and over again, "what a good boy." I grumble, eager to express that I am not a boy and flinch because mum is not amused, as she brings me back to her side, with a sharp reprimand.

Her face warms up with white sunlight, as a delicate smile lifts her eyes, making them shine, as the tall oak tree looms its familiar shadow, beside the dark, silhouette of the village stocks which hold grim memories that are deeply ingrained in their tortuous past. We take steady steps to the front of the bus as it jolts and shudders before grumbling to a stop. The folding doors hiss open, mum jumps down to the cold, hard pavement and stands still to find her bearings in this unknown place while dizziness fogs her mind and her balance falters with my soft leather lead held tightly in her hand. She gains reassurance when she strokes my back, while she slides my working harness over my head.

The bus pulls away leaving behind a dark grey cloud of smelly fumes, as we begin to find our direction. The atmosphere is still and quiet here, except for the local wood pigeons that croon broodily, as if to wake everyone that is still under the protection of their warm blankets. It is only nine thirty, early enough for someone to be cooking smoked bacon and fresh eggs. The wonderful smell lingers around a cottage nearby. When I investigate the delicious aroma further, mum pulls me back to concentrate on the route ahead.

The roaring engine of a car with a thumping-exhaust races by, blowing toxic fumes in my face. Mum is startled by the noise and stops quickly, to catch her breath, cross that she has been rudely disturbed from her daydream.

I sniff the local grass verges, edged with sticky mud while she finds her tall, agile balance, by touching the dry-stone walls that frame beautiful gardens. The sweet fragranced honeysuckle trails boldly along the walls in yellow drifts while humming bumble bees gather its sweet nectar. Purple lavender bushes burst with their medicinal aroma, as we brush against their gentle fronds, tall golden grasses tickle my nose with spiky seed heads.

These gardens are full of many varieties of scented roses, in blushing pinks. Paved garden paths are scattered with bursting displays of cottage garden flowers, leading up to brightly painted front doors that seem welcoming for all. Mum runs her awakened hands, along the rough garden walls, to feel the heat ingrained in the healing stones while I chase the air with my nose, to follow the strong-musky scent of a territorial cat that peers out at me, from underneath a parked car.

A narrow road with a slight curve leads my attention while mum is finding the way by searching for landmarks. Suddenly I remember where to go, so I straighten my back, stand taller and slightly pull on the harness, until it feels tight around my chest. I can smell those wonderful meadows, almost taste them on the tip of my tongue. I want to get there as quickly as I can. Mum asks me to take it steadily, as she is feeling every hard pull with her shoulders. I can smell the thick, black circles of steaming cow-pats, that have fallen on cold-mud, the strength of odour makes me whimper with excitement. I encourage mum to walk on faster, until I make her stop at a gap in the stone wall, where an old-wooden kissing gate, welcomes us both into the open field.

My high-pitched, tuneful whine pleads with her to let me go while I eagerly push my wet nose down on the grass, to savour the most pungent of all exciting smells. Mum releases my harness with a smooth sweep and secures my best red play collar around my neck, equipped with a bell that just increases my quivering excitement. Although I want to run, I sit upright tightly motionless, to wait for my command, ears twitching and mouth drooling eagerly. Mum strides ahead, totally ignoring me as the cows watch calmly in the next field. She turns around to face me directly and states cheerfully "off you go," which sends me, straight off like a bullet from a gun.

That burst of powerful energy, as I shoot out of a sitting position, is fierce. I run to explore the plethora of scents in this meadow of freedom, although I always turn back to mum, to check she is alright and then dash off again, knowing that my jingling bell is an excellent signal to let her know that I am close by if she needs me. Will she need me?

We reach the open waters of the river Stour, that flows beside St Mary's Church. We stand closely together, to soak up the atmosphere of this sacred space, although with a growing feeling that mum is too close to the water, I stay beside her, desperately wanting to jump in for a swim. She puts me back on the lead and listens to my whining voice while we take in the gently-flowing river, that stretches out towards a primitive wooden bridge. In the background, the cabbage aroma of the heavy cows is comforting, while the lethargic thud of their hooves shakes the ground with every slow step. A light weight aeroplane hums overhead, detached from the earth completely, while the brass church bell strikes ten 'o' clock.

Mum releases the lead and I take a golden opportunity to jump straight into the sparkling water, with a huge "splash." I find that the river is surprisingly cold. I make good progress to the other side of the bank, until my paws become stuck in a tangle of pond weed. The more I wriggle, the more the weeds twist and tangle around my legs. Mum wades out to rescue me and hooks my lead onto my collar, as the river begins to deepen, she untangles my paws quickly then strongly pulls me through the tall water reeds and dense grasses. We disturb a mother duck and her family of ducklings, who scatter with sharp, reprimanding quacks.

Removing the water from my shiny coat, takes many rough and ragged shakes, as I act like a wild beast, with gleaming bright eyes, content to fan mum mercilessly with spray. She glares in my direction, with a grey fog around her head, as she squeezes out her dripping wet jacket that is covered in smelly pond weed. We both look at each other, the guilty expression that I wear in my large, dark eyes causes mum's face to light up with an easy smile. The grey fog lifts to my huge relief, as she begins to laugh out loud loosely while she reaches down easily, to unfasten my lead because she aches no more. We run together, past the startled cows until we reach the kissing gate, where mum always thinks of new love.

I pant loudly, as I work steadily along the winding lane. The white harness weighs heavily on my back, it slips awkwardly against my wet coat, as I guide mum's gentle hand very slowly, to the quiet bus stop that feels so still, that it must surely be frozen in time. Although the lazy sun waits patiently here, to warm and dry us while mum leans heavily to rest against the dry-stone wall, in her old daisy boots while waiting for the welcoming bus to pull up beside us.

The tired driver opens the door, where the heat that hits our faces is welcoming, as she allows us in with a smile in her voice, before she glances behind her to check that all of her passengers are seated. Happy that all is well, she continues her journey to take everyone back to their home town.

The healing moon

The moon, in the major arcana of the tarot shows that a situation is not what it appears to be on the outside. Don't dismiss the feeling that you can help loved ones that are trying to hide a problem, be aware that the psychology of others is more complicated than you realise. You can nourish the strengths of others, so that their weaknesses fall into the background and their beauty shines through.

The moon demonstrates this scenario while it is visible between chasing clouds on this warm, summers evening. A young woman stands under the moonlight. With earthly vibrations calling, she feels free to express the beauty of her curves. As she touches the moon beams that are exquisitely transferred to her body, her skin tone changes with touch, it becomes warm and delicately tender as the muscles loosen and the skin releases its tightness. The new plumpness and supple quality of her skin, allows for lines and deep creases to be smoothed and softened. Influenced by the moon cycles, she becomes alive with feminine sexuality, enhanced at this time by her fertile body, she glows radiantly. She has been waiting for this release, this special time just for her. Tonight, she appears effortlessly powerful, yet submissive as she is there as an energetic strength. There is a release captured here that cannot be ignored, as a radiant expression of aura vibrations resonate throughout her being, under the healing moon.

She celebrates her transformation from a free-spirited girl, who remembers growing up to become a woman, who shares her desires as a lover. Then nurtures the loving responsibility of a mother, who knows her own mind.

Take the next step

There is no comparison to the heavenly bliss of your partners hands on your tired shoulders. Sharing your recovery with another, is the permission you give for a loving partnership to exist. Think about your partner as you choose a new angel number. This is only the beginning of a beautiful sensory journey.

Angel 29 of Reality

The angel of reality is number twenty-nine, he shows you that everything you can imagine is possible when you push away fear. Surely when the fear is gone, you are in charge and indeed, you write the rules to your own reality.

Angel number twenty-nine shows you how you can face up to reality, by pushing away troublesome fears that stand in the way. They try to stop you from living the life that you really want to have. Although you must remember that fear prevents you from coming to harm. A fight or flight response that prepares you to escape from danger, or fight your corner if the need becomes necessary.

Turn back to find the answers

A powerful visualisation about a special time in your life that begins when you Imagine that you sweep the thick dust and draping cobwebs off your old photograph album. Pull apart the stuck together pages and allow yourself to become captivated by nostalgia while you enjoy the musty, sweet aroma of the photographs. You examine the brittle, sepia negatives and continue to carefully turn the pages, back through time until you find photographs of yourself, before you had any fears that stopped your progress. You find a picture that shows you smiling and content, very much like you are going to be today.

Look at the image of yourself and work out who took the picture. Remember what that person said to you, before you heard the photographer's click, then blinked as you saw the camera's white flash. Think about who else was with you. Watch more closely and then study the picture further still. Notice that the people who are with you begin to move slightly. As you blink, imagine that their facial expressions change continuously. You can even see their lips move, as if they are talking to you. It is important to understand what is being said. The only way to hear is to be closer. Close your eyes and keep the image in your mind, bold and bright.

Allow yourself to fall into the time that your photograph was taken. The colours are bright and carry a comforting, warm glow. In this safe place, allow the aroma of your surroundings and the feelings of freedom and calm to be with you. Notice how very calm you feel now. You are genuinely content and completely free and even though you have structure to your days, you can still be yourself.

You can now understand what the people in the picture are saying to you. Although the warm, contented calm feelings are much more evident than words and as you are so reassured by the confirmation of your feelings about this time. You are released from the fears that restrict your freedom today.

As you slowly open your eyes, keep this sense of calm with you and the image of your special photograph stored safely in your mind. Whenever you want to remember how calm you really are, just close your eyes, take a deep breath and think of that special time again.

Take the next step

Move forwards without being pushed in a quiet, calm place where you can take your time. Imagine what you want in your reality while you choose a new angel number, then continue forwards to a new sensory journey.

Angel 30 of Learning

The angel of learning is number thirty, he reminds you that when you continue to fall in love with the same person, your life path together is meant to continue. The future is unknown, so you will need to help each other to learn the way and when all of your fears are overcome, you will work together confidently.

A treacherous river

So here you are with your closest partner, overlooking the stretch of river Stour between Sturminster Newton and Blandford Forum in Dorset. You look up to see the threat of heavy rain clouds hanging overhead. Both of you head towards the sound of rushing water and feel your way through sharp thorns, that tear at your bare skin. Your shorts and t-shirts proving to be little protection in this open climate.

Cautiously, you tread along the stony river bank, that has a sparkling view of the clearest water that you have ever seen, flowing steadily through fields of crops that are dotted with mature trees, ancient hedgerows and the occasional woodland copse that stretch across the green, grassy water meadows and chalk downlands of Dorset.

Your two small wooden rowing boats are waiting for you, tied with twisted rope to a leaning over tree. You shuffle along the slippery, bent over trunk. Scuffing your knees in the process and discovering that balance will take practice. You admire your partners agility and poise, as she pulls herself along the branch and elegantly drops down into one of the small rowing boats. The ability to row a boat takes skill and patience, in a slippery and rather uncomfortable environment, but with confident good humour, you encourage each other to have a go.

As you take the oars of your boats and begin to row down-stream, you keep a steady pace as the slippery oars hit against annoyingly jutting out rocks. Cold stiffens your fingers and the persistent pull of frothing water, surges up to sweep your oars away. Breathing strongly, you pull back the wooden oars against your powerful chest, as you gain focused determination, never to be beaten back at all.

You both continue the challenging journey. Shouting at each other over surging torrents. Dark clouds open overhead and rain blows into your eyes then your hearing Is distorted, so that you can't hear her voice any more.

In confusion you wait, enduring a chilled silence that stops your momentum. A heart beats pause stops your breath, as panic sets in. With a brisk glance you see that she is really struggling to push against the strong current. You see that her boat is heading straight into a whirlpool.

All help is too late, she is spinning rapidly out of control and her wooden boat capsizes, trapping her underneath. She is struggling to stay afloat, still swimming as she is sucked under water, where all around her are the cold depths of darkness.

She uses all of her strength to swim out, from underneath the submerged boat and up to bright and dazzling daylight. Gasping and blinking, fighting to swim against the force of violently churning waters. Beaten back, she is pulled under again. Her agility helps her but her strength is fading as she struggles to reach for the distorted, white shapes that appear to be swirling in the fluid darkness. With desperate hope, she stares up through the water, to the sky above. She holds close the hopeful image of a hand that reaches down to her, through the confusing turbulence of the water.

She grabs hold of the hand tightly and as you pull her free from the treacherous current. You coil up a life line rope and loop it around her body, secured under her exposed armpits. She is gasping for air as she holds on tightly to the wet rope and you pull with all of your strength. Leaning back to haul her in, you reach her heavy, sobbing and shivering body and hug her tightly. You wait to be reprimanded for not acting soon enough. Thankfully she smiles between heavy gasps of air. She is shocked and shaken, but free from the swirling vortex to the under-water world, where creatures of the deep may lurk and wait. Pools of tears leave her eyes as her shattered boat sinks forever. She is so grateful to be safely with you and watches admiringly as you row strongly towards the river bank.

She smiles gratefully when you cover her with leaves to keep her warm. Then you set about gathering sticks and dry leaves to build a primitive fire. She removes her glasses and focuses the sun's rays through a clean lens to ignite the brittle leaves. A single flame is the start of a good, hot fire. Huddling together to keep warm, you both realise how vulnerable you are. Yet how strong you are to survive this challenge together.

Judgement

Judgement, in the major arcana of the tarot shows that you have worked incredibly hard to get this far. The conclusion to a major project is in sight, although you must take a step back to check the finer details of your work. If you have exams coming up, take yourself to a quiet place. Slow down each breath and when you are calm, visualise yourself in the examination hall with your paper in front of you. Imagine that you have learnt enough to complete all of the questions efficiently. Know that you are capable of achieving your target grade, just focus on your own space, let everyone around you fade into the background then ask the angels of learning to help you. Imagine that you have finished the exam paper, you have completed all of the questions to the best of your knowledge. Understand that you have done all that you can and thank the angels of learning. Now you must relax then take some time for yourself with a reward for your efforts.

Take the next step

All good partnerships have special memories and continue to change. Choose a new angel number that is associated with your partnership, then take the next step to a new sensory journey.

Angel 31 of Love

The angel of love is number thirty-one, this masculine and feminine angel teaches that love is the ultimate treasure. It Is there for you when you believe that you are lovable and respond with the correct kind of love to other people. Take time to care for animals and look after nature with respect, then you will be rewarded with a beautiful life. Being with others allows your expression to flow with love, in the most unexpected of places.

Love at the coffee shop

The coffee shop at Ferndown in Dorset is inviting on this rainy day and as you are cold and wet, is incredibly welcoming. As the light shines through, you push the large glass doors open wide, immediately the aroma of warm coffee fills your senses, making you feel hungry and thirsty, all at the same time. While you quietly linger in the que, the comfortable conversation of others around you sounds like music to your ears.

A movement catches your eye and you glance to see the intriguing posture of a couple, sitting near the counter who are completely absorbed in deep, quiet conversation. They keep their legs tucked underneath country dining chairs, as they lean in towards each other. In that instant, they seem to be shy of their prolonged gaze which may change everything that they mean to portray. She smooths her blonde hair out of her face while he watches with admiration. You feel the magnetism of the young man's intentions while catching the scent of his sweet, musky aftershave. Feeling rather awkward, you look away from this intimate moment.

The smiling barista asks what you would like to drink, while looking at you over steamed up glasses. The young man with fine, blonde hair mixes something that smells like vanilla, as he prepares your hot chocolate with great care and attention while his work colleague pumps milk from a hot tap and her friend sprinkles marshmallow toppings on top of the frothy drink. He seems to be the only man with a few mature ladies, who are busily bustling around to make different sweet blends of coffee. You admire how they communicate so easily with each other.

The atmosphere is charged with contentment which you enjoy, as carefully you sit down on a comfortable chair and sip the cream from the top of your tall glass of hot chocolate. As you relax back, you hear a whimpering cry. You glance over to the soft lamp light in a quiet corner, that outlines the shape of a new born baby, searching for his mother's milk. A lady with a pretty smile and 'just out of bed' brown hair, that reaches her shoulders, cradles the new baby that is tucked under a very soft, blue-ribbon blanket. Her right breast is full of milk and her baby is bundled up closely, hungrily feeding, until she is completely emptied of every last drop. With a huge sigh, she swaps him over to relieve the aching tenderness of her engorged breast. The baby pauses to look up at her with bright blue eyes while she droops a sleepy stare, with doting tenderness.

Across the room are an animated group of young people, with casually placed coffee mugs and scattered side plates, that contain the crusts of sandwiches and crumbling remains of cakes. The long table is a platform for the dramatic work colleagues, who squeak chair legs and slam their fists on the table, to spark each other's imaginations with new ideas. When they settle down, they speak with low voices that contrast with sudden, enthusiastic chatter when they are satisfied with their progress.

Then there are old friends sharing their rose oil perfume, with deep conversation about who has died recently. As you listen to the clicking of their needles and continuous chatter, you realise that they are two ladies of the town, who are well known and loved for their support for local charities. Their long woollen coats are decorated with silk scarves, to accessorise their sophisticated look. The lady with short, silver hair glances up from her knitting, to sip a frothy cappuccino with hot milk. She is well respected in the community, demonstrated by her poise that holds a knowing authority. They laugh in between talking while she leans elegantly towards her friend, who's dark, shiny hair is swept behind an ear, just to make sure that she doesn't miss a word.

They don't notice the raised brow of a distinguished, elderly gentleman wearing a trilby. The hat causes a brilliant smile to light up like magic, on the plump cheeks of a little girl. She glances at him while walking past, wearing white socks and a gingham dress. She holds her father's hand, who in turn peers down and smiles affectionately at his daughter. As you notice them pass by, you stand up slowly and push the chair under the small, round table. You finish the hot chocolate then leave with the thought that love is passed around in many different forms and everybody can feel its soothing influence.

The entwined lovers

The lovers are depicted in the major arcana of the tarot by two people, who are discovering that their nakedness and mutual permission to explore the power of touch, helps them to develop a deep soul connection with each other. Their communication is at one with nature, balanced and complete.

This relationship is demonstrated by the mystical tree-people, who are linked in a warm embrace as dusk falls upon their naked bodies, breathing slow and heavy whispers. The deep and rasping breaths of the elderly beech tree in the secluded village of Ropley, can be heard clearly, as he creaks and groans in agonising pain, while the burden of his distorted boughs weigh heavily on his twisted and layered trunk, that is clothed in cracked bark that is randomly dotted with silvery knotted holes, that appear to be watching eyes. His rounded leaves are framed in silhouette form against an eerie purple sky, that descends heavily to rest over his fanned-out branches that extend upwards, to touch the heavens.

The evening birds pause their song and take flight, as the ancient boughs begin to turn and shift their silver shapes slowly, to imitate the flesh, blood and bones of human forms, that creak awake from the deepest slumber. Crooked branches groan in a long-drawn-out whine, as very slowly the shape of a woman forms, who has inward curves that fan out into gentle arched crescents, that appear as smooth and slender legs. The sleeping twilight sculpts her eyes, that appear to open brightly, when the play of light beams through hollows, channelled through her wooden head by the great spotted woodpecker.

Shadows cast their moving patterns over the creaking silhouettes, to stretch the shades of grey, to elongate the form of a man. He raises his grotesque head, that distorts into horrifying twists that shape his ragged jaw line as he tenses in pain. His jagged hands have been torn by the howling winds and bleed trails of amber sap as he sweeps rough twig fingers, across the woman's hollow face. She opens her dry, gaping hole mouth to drink thirstily from the blood of his agonising wounds.

The movement of their contorted branches, binds the lovers in their quest to discover a place, where they can merge their sensual forms. The setting sun moves dark shadows across her wild, twig hair and elongated abdomen that tingles, with the damp warmth of the sweet syrup that enlightens magical, surging waves of new growth within her. The life force of the tree carries these waves of motion, through the layers of the awakened trunk, all the way down to feed the enormous tentacle roots, that are anchored into the bed of crumbling soil.

The ancient beech tree begins to heal over the lovers with fresh bark, as the man passionately caresses his true love with his ignited form. He can feel her warm flesh and blood, so angrily fights back the healing bark that stems the flow of sap. He peels the new layers away from his bleeding hands fiercely, because he knows that their love is open, wounded and alive with the raw sweet sap of freedom, that allows them to tremble with each tingling touch, that is empowered with the flow of his pain. Hypnotised by her living soul, he pulls her mystical tree branch body closer still, until they are completely entwined.

Suddenly feeling exposed and craving renewal, she gives permission to the beech tree, to allow the healing bark to creep over their vulnerable feet, to wrap around their entwined legs, then to cocoon their bodies that cool and slow until they are completely still. As the tree-people fall asleep, their chests merge together as one and sink deeply into the supporting boughs of the beech tree, while their heads lean together, the new bark closes over the gaping wounds on the rigid, twisted hands of the man that are bent and defeated. As the sap dries like amber glass, their eyes darken and their bodies become clothed in sculptural bark, as they fall into the deepest slumber.

Take the next step

Think of an angel number to find out where your love needs to be at this present time, then turn to your new sensory journey to discover who really needs your love now.

Angel 32 of Finances

The angel of finances is number thirty-two, she highlights the need to work with another, so that you can create projects together then enjoy the process of completion and financial gain.

A message for dreamers

A hypnotic daydream, to inspire creative productivity while you explore the countryside of Four Marks in Hampshire. This landscape holds an enchanting quality, as you wander the winding roads while a cooling breeze soothes the intense, afternoon sun which warms your back, as you follow a rough farm track that leads into a never-ending bright, corn field. You follow a freshly mown footpath that surrounds the edges of ripe, golden ears of corn. Rattling as they blow forwards in waves, they share their space to dance with scattered red poppies, that make friends with shy, blue corn flowers. As you approach an orchard of trees, you rest on an old wooden footpath sign that has number thirty-two carved into the weathered post. You wonder what the significance of this number is, as you tread carefully into the woods to look for an answer there.

Now you are surrounded by the authority of trees. The tallest and most magnificent of all live in a circle, around a still, clear natural pond. A bright life source that exists in the cool undergrowth of bracken and thorns. You find a sheltered resting place overlooking the reflective pond, between enormous, living tree roots that could be compared to the arms of a chair, covered in a thick moss carpet. You settle down and relax enough to mould your shape against the tall, supportive trunk. This tranquil place allows you to close your tired eyes. Suddenly wide awake, you sharply catch your breath while you grab for something to hold your weight, scraping your hands, as you try to stop yourself from falling.

You dare not move; you are inside a tunnel that is tall enough for you to stand up in. You become aware of tall, dark shadows that appear to sweep past like shapes of robed men, gliding across the cold, compacted mud floor. The shadows are cast by the candle light lamps that hang from tree root walls. A door made of woven branches creaks open slowly, then swings closed behind you, leaving a shuddering breeze. It provides a breath of fresh air, a relief from the damp and musky odour of this underground tunnel, that you appear to be stuck in. Maybe you should go back, although you are intrigued to pick your way through jutting out tree roots, as you place careful footsteps forwards, while you cautiously feel your way, until your feet find some smooth, freshly sawn log steps, built into the earth, with bannisters that are made of cleverly twisted, woven together branches.

As your feet touch the cold, mud floor you discover that a small, circular room has been hollowed out underneath the tree. Shaped by long roots that take on the form of living beams. You smell the blended aroma of lavender, rosemary and sage.

Two ladies, are busily tying bundles of herbs with rustic twine. They sort and hang them carefully, on a drying rack that is attached to the beams. There is a large inglenook fire place, lit with the welcoming glow of tall flames that flicker, as if in conversation with each other.

The ladies Invite you to stand on the fire side rug, close to the heat. They have a special energy, you watch in fascination, as their energy glints and flutters erratically, casting translucent colours.

The younger lady with a gentle face, gestures to you to sit down in one of the two fire side chairs. She takes a black kettle off the fire hook, to brew passion flower and mint, in an old tea pot. You gratefully accept the refreshing tea then apologise for disturbing them.

The mother briskly mentions in her soft lilting tone. "Don't you worry, you are not the only one to fall through my door, but do drink up, we have to collect and clean more teeth this evening." They take this opportunity to show you their rustic display shelves. You blink, then rub your eyes at the sight of polished, milk teeth. They show you beautifully shiny necklaces, made out of teeth that are white as pearls. Remembering what you came for, you ask "Is number thirty-two on the sign post the number of your home?"

The older lady looks directly at you, with even brighter colours glowing, as she speaks with gentle wisdom. "It has a simple meaning, work with another, so that you can create together."

You begin to feel heavy and very relaxed then close your eyes. You sink deeply into this most comfortable of all arm chairs, a while later you drift awake while watching the canopy of leaves above your head. Slowly you stand up and brush yourself down. Feeling disorientated, you run your hands behind your back to find the woven door. You push all the way around the sturdy tree, although there is no give and the forest floor remains firm, cold and undisturbed.

Still drowsy, you sit down again and daydream about a small boy, who has fallen asleep while waiting for the tooth fairy to visit. The smell of angel's breath, as you watch the small boy sleep while he holds his soft toy rabbit close to him, wrapped up in the smell of fresh linen and his mother's love. His precious, clean and shiny tooth is next to his damp head. A yellow moving light grabs your attention, just behind his pillow. You see a small, white flickering movement, reminiscent of candle light. When you look again, a bright, shiny coin has replaced the treasured, tiny tooth for him to find in the morning.

Take the next step

Finances are only numbers, payment in kind and sharing are also worth so much. Sketch your plans and even make a model of what you want to achieve. Imagine living the life that you want and never doubt your capabilities. Choose an angel number for your plan then use this number for your next sensory journey.

Angel 33 of Spontaneity

The angel of spontaneity is number thirty-three, he shows that you have mastered your subject, which means that added potential for achievement is available to you, due to the twin pairing of the same number. A symbol of two special teachers, not necessarily in the formal context, teach with empathy, your knowledge is needed now, so don't hide your light away.

The blue satin-ribbon

This simple exercise allows you to be in the hands of chance, with a positive focus this chance might lead you down a path that you would not follow otherwise. By randomly choosing books, you are shown the way by using your intuition.

Imagine putting your hand on the cold, metal push plate of a heavy, wooden door. Push it open, then walk in to the local library in Blandford Forum. Smile at the busy librarian, with grey-blonde hair falling over her elegant face, as she peers down to finger through piled up paperwork, that is building up, underneath the large imposing desk.

You inhale the apple orchard aroma of old books, new paper and ink while you relax in this warm room, with towering shelves that enclose you in a space that is quiet, except for whispers. You take your time to leisurely walk along the rows of well used books and imagine the stories being read out loud.

You notice a gentle light shining through a book free gap, so glance as you pass a seated lady. She wears a high collared rain coat, with a head full of dark curls that tumble down to rest on her shoulders. Her knowing posture tells you that she is an exhausted mother, taking some time for herself at last.

You find a subject that you love, which happens to be a gripping thriller, the latest in a series that has captivated your attention for months. You open this well-made book just by bending a page. Feeling excited, you climb into the story, pretending that you live in its dramatic intrigue and as you are always on a mission, you can easily climb out of the absorbing text. You reach into your bag and find a frayed, blue satin ribbon to mark between chapters then carry your precious cargo, tucked into your side. You amble past well-loved rows of intriguing biographies and you run your loose fingers along the tempting spines, bound with textured card and laminates. Some worn, wrinkled and loose, others smooth and tight backed, thickly bound volumes. Illustrated showcases stand tall and proudly to attention.

As if you are using your mind to see, you stop at two books and pull them out to fall into your open hands. Refusing to look at the shiny cover pictures, you breathe in the sweet apple orchard aroma and smile at the blonde librarian, who looks up at you, from under her long eyelashes, as you lie the books flat on the reception desk. Passing the time of day with her, reveals a friendly mischief in her expression, that is positively infectious. You thank her, breathing out as you walk away, leaving the library behind as you grasp the cold, metal handle of the heavy wooden door and inhale the chilled, crisp air while you blink in the startling daylight, that feels like another world.

Take the next step

Take your finger off the pause button, then decide on a new angel number for your next sensory journey. Press play, as you step forwards.

Angel 34 of Change

The angel of change is number thirty-four, she moves quickly, so take notice while you can. She shows that you know yourself well and must take time to adapt to change in your own way. You are becoming more confident with expressing your true feelings to other people. Use this ability to be open for discussion and listen to the way you speak, learn quickly that communication skills bring about change for the better.

An iron-age fort

Badbury Rings, near Kingston Lacy gardens in Dorset is open and beautiful. If you can't get there, imagine that you can, and this is how it will be.

Just imagine that you are standing at the top of an iron-age hill fort, taking in the atmosphere of breath-taking space and light. Your mind whispers slow down, as you stand and open out your arms to sheer space, so you feel like you can fly. Now your body is asking you to listen while you are at the peak of three rolling hill forts, iron-age sculptures formed in the land, chiselled expertly to make waves of rolling walls, that spread out across a vast area, like constantly moving ripples across the ocean.

You think about the fathers, husbands and sons who worked hard to protect their families, inside the security of the villages. Imagine that you can hear the chinking of ancient metal tools, the farm yard sounds of livestock, children laughing and women talking in the language of a time long past.

Cavernous valleys dip steeply for many miles, an alien landscape with a stunning atmosphere, that seems like a dream. The ground begins to roll and change as you move towards the trees. Breathe and relax, as you watch the sharp, chalk definition on the edge of the rings, that is highlighted brilliantly at changing angles. Sheltered by woodland, a panoramic name plate is proudly showcased on a stone monument. Carved into the metal plate are names of towns and villages in Dorset. Arrows point you towards them and the distance to walk to each place is shown when you choose a destination.

You will find that this is the most spiritually busy and historically intriguing place. Here, you may want to listen to your life changes when they call you. Breathe and relax, stop chasing yourself away, with the changing weather patterns sweeping dark clouds over the ridge waves, allow yourself to change.

The happy Fool

The major arcana of the tarot suggests that the fool hides in images that are created with sweeping dreams of burnt orange and green. A restless woman attempts to get a good night's sleep. Instead, disturbing dreams swirl around her in the darkness. Large feminine eyes watch her from the night time window and a family in spirit are murky shadows standing at her feet. They all want to communicate with her and she knows it, she also realises that her learning is to be in control of these people in spirit, that visit her.

The fool demonstrates that challenges from spiritual beings, can be new opportunities for change. Have faith in the future and don't let unsettling experiences hold you back.

Other, more earthly beings may give you a feeling of being stifled, by too much good advice and as you have plenty of experience, be confident that you can make positive changes and start again.

Breathe in deeply and relax into your comfortable bed where nothing can bother you at all, then hold the emotions that are with you. Imagine the colour of the emotions, their texture and the feeling they give you while holding them, closely to your chest. Absorb them as you breathe and feel a sense of calm purpose while you drift into a daydream with one of your emotions, just one. With calm purpose, you can make a beautiful change to your outlook on life.

Take the next step

Change is progress in a new direction, "powerful creator, be positive with your changes." A fresh discovery may surprise you, when you choose the next angel number, that takes you to explore a new sensory journey.

Angel 35 of Solitude

The angel of solitude is number thirty-five, he knows that you work at your very best, when you have planned everything well in advance. He underlines his opinion that you can take a few risks and be brave with new ideas that you are developing, because the dust can settle for far too long. Angel number thirty-five, encourages you to polish a high shine on your project then push its potential as far as it can go. See it through to the end, even if you are not completely satisfied, ask for other opinions and you may be pleasantly surprised.

The lazy cat

An energy cleansing meditation at Hatchet Pond near Beaulieu in the New Forest. On a summer's day, escape from town life to Hatchet Pond, which is just outside the village of Beaulieu, if you are unable to visit today, imagine a lazy cat stretching out in the midday sun. Watch how he moves then very slowly and deliberately, copy him. Reach your hands up to the sky and stretch your spine in the same manner as the comfortable cat. Stretch your arms wide in a very natural way then bring the image of a green meadow into your mind.

You have bare feet that feel everything, as you begin to walk down the slope with gentle grasses brushing against your legs. Meadow birds call and the fresh rural atmosphere is exhilarating.

Your feet discover sandy ground and every few steps you tread on small stones and dry foliage with interesting textures, that make you slow down, as you do so become more aware of each step, as you walk down and down again until you realise that both feet are immersed in pleasantly cool water. The shingle feels damp as you bend down to feel smooth, grey pebbles that are washed to the sides. These are the treasured possessions of the pond.

Inquisitively, you lift the water to your mouth, it tastes clean and pure. It trickles through your open fingers, as you watch and compare its light to sparkling diamonds shining brightly in the sun.

The tide laps and circles your ankles, deeply pulling you in. Silently and gently enclosing you, lapping and circling deeply all the way up to your knees.

Gently, you absorb the feeling of light that you can see in your imagination. Notice the starkly bright light over the water, against the pebbles on the shore. As you compare the difference between light and dark, you take a deep breath of light into your lungs and blow the darkness out while you listen to the quiet peaceful lapping of the lakeside.

The natural elements of the water, the sun, the stones and the summer breeze all work together, gently enveloping you with a warm hug.

As you become more relaxed, your feet sink down more and more deeply still into the sand and you breathe in very slowly, then breath out to release all of the air from your body while you listen to the seagull's song while they circle again.

Chakra loving with the elements

The red energy centre creates your connection with the earth and keeps you emotionally balanced. It is called the root chakra, as you cup your hands gently over your pelvis, welcome the energy from the sand and the shoreside pebbles, that anchor you to this point in time.

The orange energy centre, moves your cupped hands gently two inches below your naval. This is the sacral chakra. Imagine you have the orange sunlight in your hands and you are shining that warm orange glow, to revitalise all of your creative expression and sexuality.

The yellow energy centre, smoothly moves your hands two inches above your naval, your solar plexus commands attention. Imagine that you hold water in your hands and trickle it through this energy centre. The vibrations from the water, flow through your fingers to boost your will power, self-esteem and confidence.

The green energy centre is located right in the centre of your chest. Think about the vibrant energy of the wind in your hands. Imagine that you can hold it and bring its life force into your heart chakra, the centre of love, compassion and self-acceptance.

The blue energy centre is lit by the light from the sky, that you hold in your cupped hands. Shine this pure blue light through the throat chakra, that exists at the centre of your throat, where the thyroid gland is located. Then think about communication and let that calling inside you become your own amplified, special voice.

The dark blue energy centre cups your hands over the centre of your forehead, and brings the depths of the lake and the tides of the moon cycles into your imagination. Give permission for this image to flow into your third eye chakra, to stimulate your intuition.

The warm, white light radiates from the crown of your head, that is home to the crown chakra and is the sum of all the lower six chakras, it is wide open to the heavens. Painted with the setting sun, the spectacular evening sky shines a single shooting star. The brightness of the white light can be held in your hands now. The dazzling trail of light loves your body, mind and spirit completely.

The hanged man

In the major arcana of the tarot, the hanged man sounds worrying, but in fact he represents solitude. Maybe you could think about taking a step back from discipline. Look at your situation while you are away from it. When everyone else appears to be getting on with their daily tasks happily, you admire them. Then you realise that in fact, this is just a mirage. A fool's game of pretence.

Everyone struggles with their daily tasks, you are not the only one. You are making your days too challenging.

This is not a punishment, just a chance to balance what jobs are important, with others that can wait. Look at this time as a blessing that will eventually bring forwards a new quality of life. When you look back, you will be grateful for your solitude.

Take the next step

Be brave as you create new ideas for the project's that you love. Choose an angel number that represents your best talent and let your positive focus guide you through the next sensory journey.

Angel 36 of Reward

The angel of reward is number thirty-six, he draws attention to dogs, that train incredibly hard to help others to keep their independence. Assistance dogs dedicate their lives to looking after disabled people with their daily life challenges. They nurture a close partnership and practice every day, to keep a good understanding of the liberating freedom of mobility.

The red chair

Join in with this dog show and family fun day in aid of guide dogs at Budmouth college in Weymouth, Dorset where guide dog Stella can see that mum is smiling while she speaks in high tones very quickly, to unfamiliar people, who need to hear about the fastest sausage eater, waggiest tail and best trick competition.

We have practised the layout of the large school hall, that I have discovered is ingrained with the smell of physical education lessons, climbing rope and parquet flooring. As we try to find the exit doors, we are spotted by the organiser, who is an extremely well-spoken, tall and elegant lady, who wears one of those long, swirly skirts that blow around my face, when she strides in front of me. She kindly takes the time to show us the way to all the facilities. When mum pauses to ask where I can run free, she shows us outside to a green playing field that I can safely explore.

Now I am happy because I have been for a good run in a new field, with all sorts of exciting cat trails. Mum ties her long, dark hair back in a ponytail, then leans down to give me my best smoky bone and my familiar bowl of clean water. I can see that she is busy, so I will have to be content. She cuddles into me while sharing my favourite bed and strokes me until I settle down. I tell her that I am fine, with a wet nudge of my nose on her blue-jeans, then turn around to curl up with my old familiar tartan blanket.

Many other smelly dogs of all shapes and sizes charge in through the large, open doors. They pant eagerly, bark and whine while pulling their red-faced owners along. Trailing wet mud on canvas shoes and wearing oversized raincoats together with summer caps.

Mum is the resident visually impaired artist today, with an ambition to paint dog portraits. Her first sitter introduces himself as a rather wet and muddy Springer Spaniel called Bertie. Mum gestures to him with her hands to sit in the large, red canvas chair. This is the biggest privilege that a dog can have while I have to make do on the floor. Mum says It was a simple idea, well it was fun and games actually, as every time his quiet owner walks away, Bertie jumps down to follow. When mum invites the shy gentleman to stay, Bertie is an absolute star, looking up at his dad lovingly for a whole half an hour. Mum is so pleased that she captured his open-mouthed and drooling pose while he had his dads undivided attention. Getting up close and personal with Bertie was worth the drama because his owner was absolutely delighted with the signed portrait that was most definitely a team effort. Soon afterwards,

Bertie won the fastest sausage eater competition, the bouncy Springer Spaniel, paraded his first place, yellow neck scarf with huge excitement and pride.

I don't mind all the attention, but I am happy to be quiet and subdued today. Work has become difficult for me too. Mum thinks that it may be time for me to retire, whatever that means and although I am in good health, mum is worried about me, because I want to go home, but stay polite, patient and tolerate every excitable dog that sniffs me. All of the pictures on display are of me, I happily allowed mum to paint my portraits and together we proudly raised a good amount of money for guide dogs that day.

I was so incredibly proud and happy to be a guide for mum. I wore my collar and guide dog's badge with dignity and my tail never stopped wagging when I worked. Soon after the show, the day came for mum to sadly hang up my working harness.

A while later, new guide dog in training Quaver, moved in with a brand-new harness and paraded a cheeky attitude around the house. I quickly formed a position of authority over Quaver and showed her that I am the boss. When she got the message,

the stiff, new white working harness onto I allowed her to share my space and that night mum found us curled up together, asleep on the same bed. The next morning, I barked as the doorbell chimed,

Mum opened the door to a guide dog trainer who handed her a new lead and harness. Mum fastened young Quaver's slender back. With her tight, new leather lead in her hand, she said goodbye to me.

My job had been taken and feeling devastated, all I could do was whine and watch longingly, as the young black Labrador Retriever paraded her working harness for the first time.

I suddenly realised what retirement meant, as I watched mum and Quaver, walk out of the door, to embark on their training together. Although my working days had come to an end, I had guided mum for seven years, with five children in tow which was beyond my call of duty. I continued to join in with the family days out and also to look after mum in my own special way.

Take the next step

What would you like to be rewarded for? Take this thought with you as you choose a new angel number then turn to your next sensory journey.

Angel 37 of Trust

The angel of trust is angel number thirty-seven, he can shake things up a bit and bring about spontaneous change that is revitalising to all areas of your life and very much needed. As people of this earth, something is stored up inside us. Its presence makes us vivid, beautiful and powerful. Our enthusiasm for excitement is a life food for each other. Express this vibrancy in your personal qualities, celebrate your unusual perspectives, not reluctantly but with the enthusiasm that your true self deserves.

Swimming with a dolphin

Find freedom at Durlston bay, Dorset and imagine that It's only a dream, just a dream as you drift like a feather, carried on the breeze. You breathe the luxurious quality of salty sea air into your lungs then very slowly, blow out all of this revitalising life force again, to be replenished with the vibrations of the sea, that fills your senses, that allow you to release your body from the tenuous grip of tension.

Now you are ready to loosen your shoulders as you tread on wet, slippery pebbles that sting and scrape your sensitive feet, before your searching toes sink onto welcoming cushions of foamy seaweed that is washed up on the flat, reflective sand.

You really appreciate the warmth of your tight, black wet suit and gasp with the shocking chill, as you wade strongly into the clear water then swim powerfully forwards, bristling with anticipation to find your dolphin friend.

You tread water when you hear a tremendous splash and feel the salty sea spray shower your face. You blink and see the silhouette of a shiny, bottlenose dolphin surging upwards. A powerful white, frothy shower follows behind as he rises out of the calm water, continuing to jump and fall, jump and fall again, in a beautiful rhythmical movement.

He raises his shiny, dark grey head and opens his mouth in a smile, a greeting that is returned with your own happiness and an outstretched hand to touch his face. Suddenly he disappears under the surface, so you look around to find him. A few seconds pass, before he nudges your feet playfully. Surprised by this show of affection, you reach out to stroke his long, sleek body and reach further still, to hold on to his dorsal fin with both hands.

The dolphin swiftly submerges you under water into the bubbling, swirling movement. Your lungs release air very slowly indeed, as you stretch out your supple body in the cool ambience.

Your body moves like it never has before while you swim alongside this beautiful creature. Your skin tingles with goose-bumps that ignite your nerves with invigorating excitement that travels all the way down, to the arches of your feet. As you feel the movement of his elegantly streamlined body, that glides and turns so gracefully while his dorsal fin slides between your thumb and forefinger, as he pulls you through the water.

You see the shimmering swirls of sunlight that penetrates the depths of the ocean, as you gracefully glide up to the surface, where you blink over and over again, then breathe in the life-giving sea air very deeply. Shaking your head vigorously as you breathe out in short, slow puffs while the dolphin playfully nudges your toes.

You fill your strong lungs and know that your body is graceful, you really appreciate the cool waves, that bring you gifts of diamonds, that sparkle and dance. They highlight your face while you breathe in very powerfully and deeply.

Your friends warm, salty breath tickles your neck, cheeks and all of your senses, causing you to laugh out loud. Then he silences you, pulling you down and down again, through the bubbling and swirling turbulence, where your light illuminate's shoals of white bait that shine brightly and shimmer while they are carried as spiralling flashes, glinting with silver tones, against subtle blue shades, that welcome you to be a part of all this beauty, that makes you feel completely invigorated.

You know that you can trust your friend who is kissing your enlightened toes, as you swim upwards. You effortlessly hear his gentle clicks, as his slippery belly rubs against yours with an awesome strength, yet with graceful ease.

He takes you down again, so that you can touch the garden of corals and shells that move and sway peacefully. On your return to the surface, you let go of the bottlenose dolphin to tread water and listen for his echolocation clicks for a while. All is perfectly silent while you realise your vulnerability for the first time. You dive under and with relief, you see the dolphins familiar nose gleaming, through a shoal of silver and white sand eel, his peaceful face is stunning.

The trusting Hierophant

In the major arcana of the tarot, trust is represented by the Hierophant. He symbolises the Pope, the spiritual father and the trinity of mind, body and spirit. He also represents discipline, organised religion and carries a message of mercy and compassion.

Trust yourself to achieve the knowledge that will improve your confidence. Then you will be able to push your abilities further. Ask for the cooperation of those in your family, who understand that you need to work, although don't forget, that they need your company too. Remember to share your dreams with your life partner, who has the key to your deeper connection with closeness and touch. There will be no more hiding from your true selves anymore.

Take the next step

Trust shines a light to illuminate the angel number of your next sensory journey. Imagine the possibilities that can open up to you, when you let go of fear. Trust that there is always someone there to be your friend, as you take the next step forwards.

Angel 38 of Souls

The angel of souls is number thirty-eight, she relates to your soul-purpose while she asks you to have the confidence, to pass on your gift for inspiring others. Share your knowledge, so that others can benefit from your point of view.

Sailing for all

This journey was made possible by the incredibly dedicated sailing instructors who give sailing lessons to the disabled at Rockley Park, Poole. The temperature is cool on the open waters, as you imagine that you are sitting aboard a sleek, sailing boat. Undulating tides splash and push perpetually, against the gleaming white sides of the boat which reflect the dazzling sunlight.

Listen to the flapping sails hush, as the vast canvas sheets harness the wind while the swelling waves rise up powerfully, to lift the boat forwards. Taste your lips that are laced with the salty sea spray then feel calm wash over you, as your soul fills with tranquil joy. All your worries disappear, as every ache is released into the chasing breeze. You work the winch lines to haul up the main sail then swing over to take the helm. The experienced sailors with you, make sure that the boat stays on course.

How empowered you are, as you guide the helm and keep in touch with the rhythm of each wave during this incredible experience. As the boat lurches powerfully forwards then heels at a sharp angle. You feel the movement of its elegantly streamlined shape, that glides and turns gracefully. The waves sparkle and dance, illuminating your face that becomes alive, as you breathe in very deeply.

A large yacht passes by, its sails tight and proud. The sound of the yacht crew talking to each other is amplified by the water and the children on their small canoes call to each other to "stay back."

The wind direction can be felt on your cheeks and helps you to steer the boat, filling the sails with graceful ease and powering the boat forwards steadily. When the wind drops, the sails hang, like wet sheets, leaving the boat stranded on still waters, until a constant gust fills the sails once more.

The feeling of weightless movement while skimming across the surface of the sea, can be compared to the many shades of sky blues, that surround you now and the combination of colours that swirl and spin on the water, as they do so, all of your heavy, weighted worries sink to the depths of the ocean bed. They are left behind there while the paler shades of blue, float up to the surface to ripple and dance and your soul reaches out to them, holds them closely then absorbs these beautiful colours.

Light weight and floating as you are now, you drift into the swaying rhythm of the boat and listen to the sails fill suddenly with a cool breeze, you watch the white sails against a pale blue sky and feel completely at peace.

Life before death

In the major arcana of the tarot, the fear of death is chased away by the sound of flapping sails which are good for the soul and the soul is constantly evolving. "All aboard," "ready about," "Lee ho." It's time to change the boat around.

Death brings about change, in other words the seasons are changing and so are you. Be aware of an enjoyable, transitional period where you become more aware of how good life is. It could be your age is playing a part in what your ambitions are now. You don't always need to be sprinting the race of life. Look at this time as an evolution that is essential for your happiness and don't be scared to embrace it.

Take the next step

New beginnings are incredibly exciting and take some careful, creative planning, so think of a new angel number and relax into your next sensory journey.

Angel 39 of Brothers

The angel of brothers is angel number thirty-nine, he invites you to look forward to meeting up with your family, for a long-awaited reunion. Plan picnics, lunch parties and outdoor camping trips then celebrate your circle of friends and family with gifts, good food and music. Let them know how very special they are with sincerity and feeling.

Angel number thirty-nine, is in relation to brothers that stand out and shine with creative expression. A brother's face shows many feelings that capture and portray his true character. He creates and finds many ways to encourage his brothers to work with him and just as importantly, Joins in with their activities. He demonstrates calm, to cool down an out-of-control situation, and genuine protective responsibility for each of his brothers every day.

In difficult times, the angel of brothers reminds the family to stick together, to cook and clean, keep listening to each other and have awareness of illness and vulnerability among them. When brothers stick together, they are true survivors.

A bed-time story

A busy camp site on a hill ridge at Thorness Bay on the Isle of Wight, where intimate tents glow with bed time torch lights. Evening camp fires burn down to smoking charcoal embers.

Content voices of many families with varied accents, blend to echo around the atmosphere.

Cradled in this cosy valley and illuminated by torch light, three boys are wrapped up in their comfortable sleeping bags. Two of them have their eyes closed. One appears to be sucking his thumb and the eldest boy, who wears glasses is completely absorbed in the text of a Greek mythology book.

A third tired boy is falling into dreams, his arms casually placed across his chest. They each give silent permission for their warm, colourful auras to merge together as one. In between the sleepy boys, the spirit of another child rests, as if he were part of the family, he reads a book quietly, his image only evident as a soft, white glow. It is possible that he visits every night.

Take the next step

If you have a brotherly figure in mind, explore the role that he plays in your life. Be grateful for his influence and think about him, as you choose a new angel number then begin your next sensory journey.

Angel 40 of Anger

The angel of anger is number forty, she has been brought to your attention because your daily routine needs to be adjusted and balanced, to give you a slower pace of life. Make a special space to sit. It can be anywhere that appeals to the child in you. Choose for yourself a park bench, or a favourite stair. Relax back on a bus journey, or whatever makes good sense, to that very important child in you.

This quality time, does not need to be measured in minutes, or hours. You make the decisions here, based on your feelings. Discipline yourself to stay in this peaceful environment until you are called away and even then, take your time and stay calm so that you don't lose the connection with the child in you.

A warm hug

You are right to think that your life repeats patterns. Anger is just one of those patterns that exists in a rich tapestry of emotions. This is a thought-provoking visualisation of anger when it is just passing through.

Inspired by the rolling hills of Milborne St Andrew in Dorset, which is a soothing environment to escape to when you need to work through that awful feeling of anger. On this occasion, your partner has upset you so much, that your emotions are all over the place as you tread through drifts of snow, lifted up high by howling, bone chilling winds that take you further and further away from her, where you can be on your own to release her infuriating presence altogether.

You try to avoid these destructive thoughts and talk to yourself, knowing that the wide-open space can listen to you, without the threat of it rising up to answer. As you walk, you stop to take in the dazzling white expanse of deep snow, as it meets on the horizon with the pure, white sky. Their union is as perfect as a freshly made bed, as if the snow and the sky have been ironed and tucked into place. Now you wait for yours and hers to be the same.

Then you imagine that the lightning rips through in fury, tearing up the perfect, white sheets of sky. In retaliation, the thunder bellows its terrifying reply. The force of the wind wails and howls in frustration while the heavy black clouds, cry like pillows of tears, releasing devastating sorrow all the way through the dark, restless night.

Still calm morning light and radiant sunshine brings harmony and contentment. The white cotton cloud pillows, caress the white cotton sheet sky, dancing and merging into one another, changing shape in their sheer weightless joy, happy to be together, until the sky rumbles with thunder once again.

You smile to yourself as you think about the forever changing sky and compare it to your relationship, until your feet sting and your legs ache, as they absorb the bone chilling temperatures. As you stride through the snow leaving a trail of deep boot prints behind. Howling winter winds and drifting snow sweep across the desolate valley.

You are grateful to reach home where you remember your mother's warm hug, a greeting where you both shared conversation about the day. There would be a hot meal that she had lovingly cooked and laid out ready for you on the kitchen table.

Although today, a warm fire is burning in the grate with cheerful orange embers on starkly black coals. Your vision blurs with tiredness, until all you can see is the jumping sparks and hungry flames that lick and crack in an understanding manner. Your fingers are red and sore with the throbbing sensation of pain, as warm blood surges back through your cold veins. All of your negative emotions are absorbed by the fire, as anything unhappy is burnt away and rises with the grey smoke, that drifts out through the chimney, in lonely signals that are carried on the treacherous, howling winds.

The cold stings painfully, like ice needles sticking into your palms, as you hold your throbbing hands up to the heat and you sit with a thick blanket around your shoulders, as your wet clothes have been abandoned like old rags, scattered around your painful feet that sink deeply into the soft, cream sheepskin rug.

With a certain amount of pleasure, you feel the sensation of movement return to every aching limb. You shiver, feeling helpless and lost without your lover's arms to hold you closely.

As your thoughts drift towards her once again, you hear the sound of her bare feet padding on the creaky floorboards and the scent of cedar wood oil brings her to you with earthly vibrations calling. She feels free to express the beauty of her curves, as she rests her reassuring hands on your shoulders firmly and slowly, lets the blanket fall while she places a soft, bath robe around your shoulders. You pull the warm, welcoming gown on gratefully, then relax back into the fire side chair with a deep sigh of contentment, as your heart warms with every touch of her hands while she blends warm oils into the tone of your skin. Her breath is warm on your back while her hands pull your masculine shoulders backwards slightly, as you begin to relax very deeply while your feet sink into the luxurious sheepskin rug. She pulls you back once again, as your energy falls onto the floor, crumpled up with the drapes of a warm, white towel that lies at her feet. She appears effortlessly powerful, as she supports you with her loving hands.

Everything makes sense now that your emotions are calm and balanced. You know that you are not complete without your loving partner, she has been waiting for you, for this special time for both of you to share. She knows that your strength will return as she releases all of the tension from your aching body. There is no comparison to the touch of your partners hands as the skin tone changes with touch, it becomes soft and tender, as the muscles loosen and the skin releases its tightness, in the gentle hands of your partner.

Take the next step

Anger is like an uninvited noisy visitor, just passing through like the queen of all drama and without balance, anger is a destructive energy storm.

Then in the calm after the storm, love brings back balance, taking its turn to chase anger away, allowing you to choose a new angel number, so that you can start the next sensory journey, leaving all anger behind you because the end is in fact, only the beginning.

THE END

About the author

Emelye with Stella on her retirement day, and Quaver on her qualification day as a guide dog.

As an artist, the human form is familiar, as Emelye uses the power of touch to create three-dimensional form. Reproducing the tactile warmth of the human body in the full flow of movement. She likes to remind other visually impaired artists to draw what they feel, not what they see.

Her first guide dog Stella was the subject for all of the dog portraits. Later, guide dogs Quaver and Arthur developed a method of working, that relied on touch and understanding. Sight loss closed old doors and while finding the way, she discovered opportunities to be expressive. Assigned to many commissions for portraits of people with their energetic dogs. She produced paintings that captured the personalities and living aura of both the dogs and their owners.

A watercolour of Stella by Emelye Purser

Emelye held a regular sensory art workshop, and taught her students to leave behind the world of perfect drawings, and immaculately detailed landscapes. Her vision showed that the detail is in the mind of the beholder.

The sensory journeys were created by Emelye when she started practising as a therapist. They are about the Dorset coast line and the Hampshire countryside. They were recorded audibly and then played back as beautiful guided meditations, to use in therapy sessions and for personal use for wellbeing and relaxation time. Ask your partner to read them to you while you have your eyes closed, because then everything is understood in a different context. One that is not obvious and that can work very successfully to help you explore the finer details of life.

She volunteered her services during the national lockdown, due to the coronavirus pandemic. She continued to support clients on video calls, to share her sensory journeys and intuitive guidance using her 'Vision Oracle Cards.'

She also gave this support to the blind and visually impaired during Wellbeing Wednesdays, at RNIB Connect South-West. These journeys were about beautiful places that Emelye translated back to others with her sensory view point.

As an Oncology complementary therapist in Reiki and massage, she works at Hambledon Health clinic in Blandford. She uses her journeys during hypnotherapy sessions, and her beautiful, hand painted cards during intuitive readings, that truly contain messages from the angels.

List of places

Peter Symond's College, Winchester, Hampshire

Cave Hole, the Isle of Purbeck, Dorset

The Bluebell Woods, Durweston, Dorset

Lucy Hill, Burley, The New Forest, Hampshire

Ringwood, The New Forest, Hampshire

Chesil Beach, Dorset

The X12 Bus to Dorchester

Bryanston Woods, Blandford Forum, Dorset

Dorchester

The Milldown Nature Reserve, Blandford Forum, Dorset

St Catherine's Hill, Winchester, Hampshire

The River Frome, Wareham, Dorset

Bournemouth Train Station, Bournemouth, Dorset

Kimmeridge Bay, The Isle of Purbeck, Dorset

Blandford Forum, Dorset

Bournemouth Gardens, Bournemouth, Dorset

The North Dorset Trailway, Blandford Forum, Dorset

Tyneham Village, Lulworth Cove, Dorset

Wareham Forest, Dorset

The Market, Salisbury, Wiltshire

The Beach House Hotel, Milford on Sea, Hampshire

Compton Acres Gardens, Poole, Dorset

Hod Hill, The Blackmore Vale, Dorset

Kingston Lacy Gardens, Wimborne, Dorset

Bridport Beach, Dorset

Sandbanks Beach, Poole, Dorset

Sturminster Marshall, Dorset

The river Stour at Sturminster Newton and Blandford Forum, Dorset

The Coffee Shop, Ferndown, Dorset

Lyeway Lane, Ropley, Hampshire

Four Marks, Hampshire

The Public Library, Blandford Forum, Dorset

Badbury rings near Kingston Lacy House and Gardens, Dorset

Hatchett Pond, The New Forest, Hampshire

Budmouth College, Weymouth, Dorset

Durlston Bay, Dorset

Rockley Park, Poole

Thorness Bay, The Isle of Wight

Milborne St Andrew, Dorset

Bibliography

Here is a list of some helpful books for you to refer to:

Ask Your Angels, A Practical Guide to Working with Angels to Enrich Your Life by

Alma Daniel, Timothy Wyllie and Andrew Ramer.

Auras, How to See, Feel and Know by Embrosewyn Tazkuvel.

Angelic Reiki: The Healing of Our Time, Archangel Metatron by Christine Core.

Angel Messages: Breathe and Lift in Angelic Love, Light and Compassion by Melanie Beckler.

Angels and Archangels in Reiki Practice. A practical guide, Haripiya Suraj.

Meditation Dreamwork by Tara Ward.

The Complete Book of Numerology, Discovering the Inner Self by David A Phillips.

Silent Awakening: True Telepathy, Effective Energy Healing and the journey to infinite awareness by Eric Pepin.

The Essential Tarot, Rosalind Simmons by Mary Hanson-Roberts.

Angel Numbers, the Message and Meaning Behind 11:11 and Other Number Sequences by Kyle Gray.

The Dalai Lamas Book of Transformation by His Holiness the Dalai lama.

Conclusion

Continue to look after yourself, in the very best way that you can. With the company of a good friend. You are valued and important. Keep making yourself available to others who need your reassurance and kind words. Thank you for sharing this journey with me, please let me know about some of your journeys too.

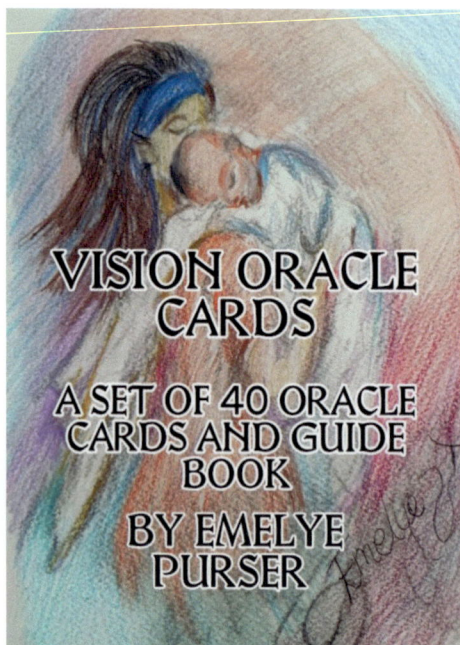

This set of beautiful hand painted, oracle cards, is complete with a guide book for assistance in all family situations. To order yours, contact by Email: emelyepurser@hotmail.com Paper copy: £25 plus postage, Ebook: £5.